Born On The Wrong Side Of The Tracks . . .

the autobiography of

Michael J. Ferrara

Michael J. Ferrara
4748 South Ocean Boulevard
Highland Beach, FL 33487

Printed in the United States of America

Cover Design by Joseph J. Palmeri
Cover Photo by Lisa F. Palmeri
Edited By Donna Ferrara, Lisa F. Palmeri and Michael Corradino

To order additional copies of this book, contact:
Xlibris Corporation
1-888-795-4274
www.Xlibris.com
Orders@Xlibris.com

To my family and friends:

I don't know what you will get out of reading my story, but I hope you will get a small percentage of the enjoyment I experienced in the writing.

This effort has drawn out for close to five years. Every day I sat at the laptop to add some information to the book, I was reminded of early life events and the effect on me today. It was a constant reminder of the blessings I received to reach my present position owning a home in Wyckoff and in Florida, with a dedicated and beautiful wife, three daughters and sons-in law, and three grandchildren.

I believe variations of the story could be written by many of you reading this book, and I hope my story will give you the confidence needed to do your own book.

I must specifically thank my daughters, Donna and Lisa, and my son-in-law Joseph for being constantly available for "obstinate" computers and a slow learning author believing a call to one of them at any hour of the night or day should be accepted.

I thank Donna for the first editing of text and Mike Corradino, my UNICO preceptor and professional editor for his subsequent editing of the UNICO Chapter and the entire text in the final days.

My son-in-law Joseph is the absolute final authority of the idiosyncrasies of the computer and the format, planning the final edition and the ultimate printing and publication of this autobiography.

The encouragement of my wife Grace to begin this effort and her patience over my years of writing cannot be expressed enough, except to say without her there would be no book.

FOR GRACE

TABLE OF CONTENTS

CHAPTER ONE

Early Childhood And School Days

I have found myself in recent months explaining why contentment has become an important part of in life. At this point (about 3:45 AM on Thanksgiving Day 2001), I thought it might be a good idea to put that feeling in print for the benefit of my children and grandchildren. The story will be only as good as my memory will permit and I am sure there will be many blanks . . . and a few embellishments. I hope readers will forgive my mistakes and lapses of memories, at least.

Without any hesitation, I can say that my life was shaped by my mother, brothers and sisters.

My mother was born in Italy on August 22, 1883. To the best of my knowledge, she came to the United States at about age 8. Her name was Anna Fruschi. Her father was Michael Fruschi (my namesake) and her mother, Madeline Pepe. I don't believe she had much schooling although she spoke very clear English, without any accent. She was very talented in dressmaking, with the ability to look at a dress in a store window, go home, cut a pattern on brown wrapping paper or newspaper and make the dress

She had two brothers. One, Rocco, was born hunch-backed and grew to about five feet tall. He lived with us a while, then was admitted to the state hospital at Greystone in Morristown, New Jersey. We made frequent visits on the weekend, taking a trolley car to Hoboken, then a train to Morristown.

Her other brother lived on Ninth Avenue between 39th and 40th Street in New York City. I believe he had five children. One, Nicky, later arranged a job for me at the New York Times. My uncle owned a movie theater with a 5 cent admission, and our big treat was free admission during our visits.

Our visits were infrequent, partly because of the difficulty in traveling with a big family. In addition to my older sisters Ida and Helen, my older brother Jerry (Sonny), my twin sister Virginia and me, my mother had to transport my younger brother Frank (Junior), born paralyzed from the hips down, without control of his bowels and urine. A trip entailed the trolley car to the Weehawken terminal down on the Hudson River and a ferry boat across the river to 42nd Street and Twelfth Avenue. Then we walked to my uncle's house.

My mother grew up in New York City and met my father there. She was working in the garment industry and he was building houses. They married in New York.

My father, Frank Ferrara, son of Gennaro Ferrara and Antonia Caputo, had five sisters and three brothers. Born in Italy around 1882, he also came to the United States in the late 1890s or early 1900s and lived in New York City.

His sister, my aunt, Carmela Ferrara Venturelli lived in Brooklyn. She had five children: Antoinette, Nicolo, Marie, Gennaro and Josephine.

Another of his sisters married a man named Michael Pergola, and their children were Joseph, Evelyn, Rita, Antoinette, Lucy, Enilda and Emily. Upon my aunt's death, the family broke up. Rita and Lucy lived with us for a while. Rita shortly went into the convent and Lucy got married. I often use this as an example of the relationship of family; that even though we were living in very limited circumstances, my mother would provide whatever shelter and food we had. Rita now Sister Mary Beatrix remains as one of my few living relations.

Uncle Mike Pergola was a barber working at the Waldorf Astoria in N.Y. On Sundays he would come to our home for dinner, and then cut our hair.

My sister Ida was born February 14, 1911. Helen was born April 27, 1914 in New York. Sometime after my father built or bought a three-story building on Broadway and 47th street in Union City, New Jersey. My brother Gennaro, always called Sonny by the family and Jerry to everyone else, was born February 8, 1918, in Union City.

On June 4, 1922, my mother gave birth to twins: my sister Virginia and me. A midwife attended at the birth, under minor supervision of Dr. Pagliughi. My brother Frank was born July 4, 1925 in Union City, with the spinal injury that left him paralyzed and incontinent. His birthday provided an excuse for a "private" use of fireworks in the very small denominations.

Around 1918 my family had opened an Italian grocery store, in a building bought with a bank loan. The building had two stores on the first floor with a three-room apartment behind each store. (In the picture, the stores have been converted into apartments.) The upper floors each had two three-room apartments.

Front of House

MJF-Virginia-Mc Glones

MJF-Virginia on lap Ida-Helen-Sonny backyard

Present Backyard Showing Dad's Addition

My parents lived in the apartment behind one of the stores. My father added two rooms which became a living room and bedroom. My parents' bedroom was three steps up from the back of the grocery store. The new bedroom was for Ida and Helen, while a dining room had a pull out bed for my brother Sonny. My sister and I slept in cribs in my parents' bedroom until my brother Frank was born. Then Virginia moved in with my sisters and I moved onto the pull out bed with my brother. When my father died, Ida moved in with my mother.

Sleeping in the dining room had a benefit for the boys in the family. There was a non-working fireplace. Every night, on its mantelpiece, a piece of pound cake would be placed by mother mainly for me but if my brother woke up he could get a piece. When I woke up during the night, I would eat the cake, brush the crumbs off the bed and go back to sleep.

My Father, Virginia, MJF and Helen in Dumont

In the summer of 1927, we had a home on Grant Ave, in Dumont, New Jersey, which my parents had planned to make our permanent home. My father became ill and died in September 1927 at the age of 45, leaving his wife a single mother with six children, aged two to 17. My mother tried to continue the grocery store but was forced to close it during the Great Depression, which began in 1929 and ran thru the thirties. Sometime in 1934 or 1935 the bank foreclosed the mortgage and my mother lost the house, for what I believe was about $900 due on the mortgage. Later, she opened a women's hosiery store.

In recalling this incidence I am reminded of the time my mother sent me to make a small payment toward the mortgage. The bank was a block away and the tellers were high and behind a barred window, and my head just about reached the counter. When I gave the teller the money he "scolded" me and said I should tell my mother if she didn't get the rest of the money he was going to take our home.(you will note I was maybe 10 or 11 years old).

Some 35 years later while I was Attorney for the Bergen County Freeholders, this man's name was offered for an appointed position on one of the County facilities. The memory was there and rather than say anything derogatory I offered the Board an alternative name saying my person was more active in our behalf. I was successful.

After my father died, Ida had to work in a dress factory. Helen went to "business school" then to work for a lawyer (and later judge) named Alfred Cozzi before she was 16. My brother and I worked on ice trucks until we graduated high school. My twin sister Virginia helped in the house and did janitorial work, washing the halls of the apartment house. My brother Junior was not able to do any work at that time.

My mother had a large factory size sewing machine in the house and made garments for a local factory. Like many families, we all helped with this "home work": putting on snaps, turning belts inside out, and other minor items required to finish the dress. When this work was completed, my brother would deliver them to the factories in New Jersey and New York City's Garment District.

The other families in our building lived in what were called cold water flats. An odd name: this referred not to the lack of hot water, but to the fact that there was no central heating. For warmth, the families used stoves burning wood, coal and later kerosene. The apartments had a bedroom, a parlor, a kitchen, and a bathroom with a tub without a shower.

Shoe Makers Building

Because of my father's improvements, we had the "luxury" of five rooms and a bath. In addition, we enjoyed a central steam heating system with a coal fire furnace in the cellar. It became my responsibility to put coal in the furnace, sift the ashes to be used for banking the fire at night, then ultimately taking the barrel of ashes out of the cellar for the garbage collector to take away.

The garbage truck was a large open body vehicle. One man would stand in the open back in the garbage and another would throw the barrels of garbage up to him. Standing in the refuse, he would empty the barrel, and then throw it back to the man on the ground. Quite different from the automated closed trucks of today!

Across the street from my house, was a shoemaker by the name of Sam Ciolino. On the side, he sold life insurance with five cents per week premium on a $500 policy. My mother may have had one for each of us. (In the picture the stores have been replaced by apartments). Becoming friends with Sam, we brought lunch over to him each day. In turn, he would repair the family shoes. If only one shoe had a hole, we had to put a piece of cardboard in that shoe until the other shoe wore out. Later, our barter system extended to include the ice, coal and kerosene I received as part of my pay for work on the ice truck and in the shoe maker shop.

In 1928, Governor of New York, Alfred E. Smith was nominated as the Democratic presidential candidate. His candidacy was met with anti-Catholic hysteria not only from familiar bigots like the Ku Klux Klan but also from allegedly respectable religious and secular sources.

Our family was part of a distinct minority in this predominantly German and Irish neighborhood. Some of our neighbors were reportedly members of the Klan or the Masons and didn't like Italians or Catholics. The prevailing bigotry had an unintentionally favorable result.

In my childhood, children could begin kindergarten in either September or February. I believe my mother lied about my birthday to get me into kindergarten in February rather than in September. My first recollections of school, however, were of the first grade.

My sister and I finished our first term of first grade; the class size had to be reduced. A new teacher, Gladys Resch (later Eberle) was hired to take the overflow. Although I believe that the other teacher did not like us or was prejudiced against Italians, we were fortunate to have the new teacher. Gladys taught us the rest of first and all of second grade.

Roosevelt Grammar School

Bob & Gladys Eberle

Gladys became my lifelong friend. She never had any children of her own but remembered every student she had taught, long after they left school. One of the kind acts she performed for my family was to arrange for a bed-side teacher for my crippled brother. At the time, schools had no accommodations for handicapped children. Thanks to Gladys' intervention, Frank not only completed grade school, he earned a high school diploma.

Through the encouragement of another fine teacher, Marie Puy, Frank learned to take and develop pictures. As a young man, he opened a professional photography studio, specializing in weddings.

It was not only weddings that Frank memorialized. During his bed-side high school, he also received what would be now called an internship with the Union City Police Department. Working in the photography department, he took and developed mug shots. When the Lincoln Tunnel was opened, my brother Frank was there to take pictures of the first cars through the underpass into Union City.

Being a photographer was not easy for Frank. In addition to his condition, technology was not user friendly. For example, before World War II, wheel chairs didn't collapse. To take pictures in a bride's house, someone (usually Sonny or me) had to carry Frank in while another dismantled the chair and maneuvered it inside. Then we'd put him back in the chair. After he took the pictures, we'd repeat the process and move to the next location.

The unfortunate injuries suffered by soldiers in World War II led to the development of folding wheel chairs, which made this process easier.

In 1946 we bought a used car and Frank learned to drive. Hand brake and throttle were necessary, of course. One impediment to Frank's getting his license was a paralysis from his hips down and he couldn't push the high beam button on the floor of the car. My brother and I made it very clear to the inspectors that if they rejected the license, there would be a news story the next day "depriving" this handicapped person an opportunity to earn a living. We prevailed.

My school career story is not as inspiring as Frank's. The grammar school was about five blocks from my home. Roosevelt School had such luxuries as a swimming pool in the basement, a large school yard with swings and a sliding pond and one basketball hoop. In the lower grades, we were able to get a pint of milk for either free or for two cents, although we had to go home for lunch.

While in the sixth grade, my future legal career was jeopardized. An appearance in Juvenile Court in Jersey City could have set me on the wrong path forever.

There was a minor snow fall in early spring. Boys being boys, a bunch of us were moved to make snow balls and throw them at a high porch wall, as if we were pitching at a baseball game.

Unfortunately, the porch was on a home owned by a true grouch. This man routinely objected even to kids playing in the street in front of his house. That day, he loudly alleged that one of our snowballs hit him in the face and broke his glasses (an impossibility even for budding Major Leaguers, because of the height of the porch).

Not surprisingly, none of us waited around to hear him out. The next day at school, the grouch and the principal went around the whole school looking for the kids involved. My 6th grade class room was unusual in size and shape. It had only three long rows of desks, with a front and side door. When the grouch came into the front of the room I hid behind the kid in front of me. It was only a momentary escape: when they went around the hall, the grouch saw me through the side door.

I was taken to the principal's office. My mother was called and a complaint was filed against me and two other kids. (Do you think today this would call for a court appearance?) Fortunately, my sister Helen worked for a lawyer, who appeared in court with us. We testified that the wall of the porch was so high and there was so little snow that it was impossible to have hit him.

We prevailed in that court, where we were innocent until proven guilty. I can assure you, however, that punishment was imposed by my mother despite the judge's ruling. In my mother's court, guilt was assessed without formalities, such as a trial. I was partially redeemed by working.

During my childhood, peddlers were common, driving around towns selling fruits and vegetables, fish, bread, ice cream etc. Most made several rounds a week. Knives and scissors could be sharpened by itinerant tinkers at least once a month. All of these vendors disappeared. Among the last to go was home delivery of milk – an occupation with which I became very familiar.

While my parents owned the grocery store, bakery and milk products were delivered early in the morning, around 5:30 or 6:00. My favorite bakery product was the long cruller, the descendant of which can still be found at Dunkin Donuts. My breakfast would also include eggs either fried, or beat up as eggnog with warm or cold milk, a drop of vanilla and in winter, hot coffee and a drop of Marsala wine.

From the tender age of seven until I graduated high school in 1940, I worked for Frank De Paola, on an ice truck at 5:30 every Monday, Wednesday, Friday and Saturday morning. In the heat of the summer, it was necessary to service the taverns on Sundays as well. During the week I returned home at 8:00 to wash, change clothes and go to school. On weekdays, I went back to the ice truck after school, not really to work but to teach Mr. De Paola to read and write as I was learning. For years, I signed his name on the few checks he received in his mostly all-cash business. (To this day, I recall him as an "old Italian man", although he was probably younger than I am now.)

While working on the ice truck, I learned how to drive. The boss permitted me to move the truck the short distance from one stop to the next and later, to take more adventurous trips.

First thing in the morning (after having a cruller and milk in the diner), we went to the ice house to load up the truck. The ice house was a very large building in which the ice was cut into 300 pound blocks. A person inside the ice house would push the blocks to a door, where we would load them on to the truck. Sometimes, I would go into the ice house to push the blocks to the door as a way of getting served when there were several trucks waiting to get their supply. It felt very nice in there on the hot summer days.

My recollection is that the blocks were about eight feet long by three feet high by one foot thick. The truck could hold seven or eight blocks. Our stops included stores, taverns and homes. In a store or tavern, we might deliver as much as a half block of ice. For some customers, we cut big pieces for ice boxes or chopped up pieces by hand.

On Saturdays, my boss had to collect payment from the many taverns we serviced. This thirsty work required him to have a glass of beer while waiting. This gave me the opportunity to become "pied piper" to my friends. To keep me out of trouble, he would give me money for ice cream sodas or other treats at each stop. As large as my capacity for sweets was, it was not hard to share it with my friends. (Of course, I was sure they were true friends having nothing to do with ice cream treats).

The barrels of beer for these saloons were stored in the cellars, with pipes running up through the floor behind the bar where the tap was connected. We had to bring the ice down the cellars and pack it around the barrels to make it cold, as there was no refrigeration. The stench of stale beer was sickening. I believe that's the reason I have never had a glass of beer or even the desire for one.

The iceboxes of the homeowners were of different sizes, which dictated how often they had to be filled. It required real expertise to cut a piece of ice just big enough to use the full area of each box. There was a drain from the box to a pan underneath that had to be emptied regularly. If you lived on the first floor of the building, you could empty the water to a cellar drain.

In the winter, the ice man became the coal man. Some houses had coal furnaces in the cellars for which we could deliver up to a ton of coal. Some had chutes, but usually, we had to fill the coal bins by bringing down 100-pound bags of coal and dumping them into the bin.

Most apartments were heated by one or more stoves. One was naturally in the kitchen and others in a living room or bedroom. In these cases, we brought a 100-pound bag of coal up to the apartment, where it was stored in a wash tub or other bin in the kitchen. My boss kept up with the times: when these coal stoves were converted to kerosene use, we would fill their small tanks on the back or side from 5 gallon containers carried up to the apartment.

In most apartments and homes, hot water was supplied by a permanent 30-gallon tank in the kitchen fueled by gas or, less often, through the kerosene stove.

Families fortunate to have a washing machine did not have to go to a laundromat. The machines had to be rolled to one of the available wash tubs in the kitchen. I don't recall any dryers back in the 1930's, except for the clothes lines from the back of the house to a pole in the yard. All the apartments in a building used the same pole for their separate lines. Drying time, of course, depended on the weather.

Part of my ice truck job was to help the boss repair his 1929 truck or 1927 Packard Touring car on Sunday afternoons. Frank De Paola lived on 68th street (was previously 24th) in Guttenberg.

Along with the ice truck, I sold the Saturday Evening Post, which, despite its name, came out on Tuesday. Each Tuesday, I left at 6:00 AM to go down to the West Shore ferry in Weehawken to sell the Saturday Evening Post along with the Ladies Home Journal. I'd return to the ferry in the afternoon to try for the commuters I had missed in the morning. I would hold up a copy of the magazine and say please buy my last copy even though I really had other copies to sell . . . just a little salesmanship. An added benefit to this job was the company's promise that if I sold a certain (enormous) number of subscriptions, I could earn a college scholarship. My mother's concern was that I would wear out my shoes trying to sell that unattainable number.

On one occasion, after selling the magazine by the ferry, I played with my friends around the piers instead of going straight home. I slipped and fell in the Hudson River. In an attempt to avoid getting into real trouble with my mother, I went into the railroad turn house (where they turned the locomotives around to go the other way) to dry. I lied to my mother, saying that I had been busy selling the magazine, which I am sure she didn't believe.

During the summer months, it was not unusual for me to stay down at the West Shore ferry after the morning rush hour until the afternoon at 3:30 or 4:00 PM. One of the ways we passed the time would be to sneak across the river on the ferry (evading the two cent fare) to New York City. We would walk up 42nd Street to the 8th Avenue area. There were many movie houses and food stands. At some stands, you could buy a hot dog for five cents and get a free jug of root beer.

There were also the Horn and Hardart Automats, where you could get anything from a donut and coffee to a full meal. This ultra modern establishment had a wall of dispensing machines with glass doors standing about three feet high. You would turn the shelves of various foods to the one you desired, then would deposit several nickels (most items were about 15 cents). The glass would open permitting you to take the food out.

In some instances, we were able to get into one of the movies for 10 or 15 cents and as I recall, they were not X rated. My Uncle's theater had long since closed and was converted to an Italian food and fruit store. I continued the magazine job, along with my ice truck job until I graduated from high school.

On some Sundays and holiday, relatives came to our house for dinner. Early in the morning, my mother would begin making the tomato sauce. The first things in the pot were onions and tomato paste, which had to cook a little, followed by the tomatoes. On Sundays, the sauce was started before we went to 9:00 AM Mass. When we returned and the sauce had been cooking for an hour, it was ready for dipping a piece of Italian bread into the pot. As an added treat, there might be meat balls or sausage added to the sauce.

It was easy to convince my mother that we were too hungry to wait for dinner to eat. This was especially true on Sundays when we had to fast from midnight in order to receive Communion. Guests would arrive around 1:30 or 2:00 PM, as Helen would be playing the organ and Ida and Virginia would be singing for the 11:00 and 12:00 Masses.

Dinner would start with some antipasto and soup, followed by pasta, such as "sewer pipes" (rigatoni), bows, linguine, perciatelli, ravioli or gnocchi. Often, the pasta would have been homemade the day before, rolled, then laid out on the bed or table for drying. The meat balls, sausage, pork, and bracciole (rolled steak filled with parsley, cheese, eggs or other stuffing) from the sauce would be followed by veal cutlets, other beef, or chicken.

While the dishes and pots were being washed (usually by the women), the table would be cleared, then set with cups and saucers for dessert, my favorite part of the meal. This could be Italian pastries, cheese cake, cookies or homemade cake. Nuts and fruit would follow. The coffee might be espresso or cappuccino or some of my mother's coffee. The coffee was made in a large pot with coffee grinds dropped into the bottom. It would be left to boil and remain on the stove all day until finished.

Brother Jerry in Parade

The men and some of the ladies and sometimes the children would play a card game, for pennies supplied by the adults. This meal would normally be finished around 5:00 or 6:00. The relatives would depart, leaving us to whatever homework was required for the next day.

In addition to the good food my mother provided, we were fortunate to have a party line phone. This shared service could have up to 6 families using a single line, but in our case, I believe there were only two or three families.

During those early years, my family got involved with St. Rocco Church in Union City. As I mentioned, my sister Helen played the organ, and Ida and Virginia sang in the choir. Jerry was an usher and later became President of the Holy Name Society. This was a major organization of the church at that time, with a full scale parade being held the second Sunday of October every year. Even I was an altar boy, learning to read and recite the prayers in Latin which was used at Mass at that time.

1936 To 1940

About 1936, we moved to a first floor apartment on 34th Street in Union City. There was a fire house across the street, which proved to be a tremendous asset. The firemen became good friends of our family. On duty 24 hours a day, they carried my brother Junior up or down the porch to the car (borrowed from a friend until after the war when he got his own).

In addition, in those days, the door of the firehouse didn't close automatically. If a fire occurred during a winter night, my brother Jerry or I would get up and go across the street to close the doors. When they returned from a fire and I was home, I would help them wash and roll up the hose.

In the early 1930's, there was a major fire at St. Michael's Monastery at three in the morning. I went to the site and helped pull hoses, etc. for several hours, bringing hot coffee and donuts to the fire fighters. As is too often the case, school interfered with the fun of being a young entrepreneur, junior firefighter and Pied Piper of the ice cream set. I had to go to high school.

Union Hill High School was one of two in the city. Students from south of 32nd Street went to Emerson High, and those who lived north went to Union Hill. This division created a major football rivalry for Thanksgiving Day. The day was preceded by street rallies and parades.

At the end of the game, the victor tore down the goal posts and paraded through the Emerson part of the city as well as the Union Hill section. Turkey dinner tasted better if you won.

Union Hill was located between Hudson Ave and 38th and 39th Streets, five blocks from where I lived on 34th Street and New York Ave. Nearby, at 38th Street and New York Ave was the Hudson Burlesque which drew many visitors from other parts of New Jersey and even from New York. In high school, I had a number of required courses for a diploma and elected to take Spanish for two years with Miss Buongiorno, one of my favorite teachers. Out of school, she hired me to do odd jobs around her house. One of my favorites was beating a rug hanging over a pulled clothes line. Though it may seem odd, I thought this was great. I would imagine I was hitting a baseball.

Rug beating was not the only way I enjoyed America's Sport. In high school, I ran a baseball pool the first two months of the season. In this pool, a person had to choose three players who would get a total of 6 hits on a particular day. If they did, I would pay them three times their bet. This was not an easy game to win: it was in the beginning of the season before anyone got a feel of the players. When my mother learned about this, I had to convince her it was not really gambling. After all, I argued, they "couldn't win".

I don't think she believed me, but my use of the proceeds to buy shoes, clothes and other necessities helped my position.

Socializing took less controversial forms. I was one of a group of boys who decided to set up a club named the Hudson A. C. We had a store front club house on 39ᵗʰ Street and Hudson Avenue, one block from the high school. We gathered old furniture and a ping pong table. Our club house provided a place to hang out at lunch, after school and at night time. Later, we formed a basketball team and ran raffles to raise money for uniforms and jackets.

Still, due to my work schedule, there was little time to get involved with organized sports. I did play on the baseball team as a catcher for some time and was a water boy for the basketball team.

This was the era of the New Deal. During the summer, the WPA (Works Progress Administration), a federal program for development, would arrange block dances with live bands. These were always fun as well as an opportunity to meet girls and boys from other towns. This was the era of big bands. Among my favorites were Tommy Dorsey, Glen Miller, Benny Goodman, Jimmy Dorsey, Artie Shaw, Duke Ellington, Vaughn Monroe, and Guy Lombardo and singers like Frank Sinatra, Perry Como, and The Mills Brothers.

On the more serious side, I was in the Debating and the Spanish clubs in sophomore, junior and senior years. The top student in the Spanish Club was Eddie Leone whose skill was helped by his subscription to a Spanish newspaper. When he graduated, he went to Marquette College in Wisconsin and became a dentist. He remained in Wisconsin, married and had a family. Many years later (sometime in the 1960's), he became a member of the Milwaukee UNICO Chapter, and we renewed our acquaintance at UNICO National conventions.

Another thing I remember about high school was the speeches by public officials and prominent businessmen who were invited to address the assembly of the student body. Of these, I recall one speaker who stated that if students could retain their inquisitiveness and alertness of that age, it would prove to be very helpful in life.

Until around 1940, a primary mode of public transportation was trolley cars, which were powered through a wire from a reel on the back of the car to an overhead line. Kids would try for a free ride by hanging on the reel. This was a fine means of getting around if you were not caught by the conductor. The primary means of evasion was jumping off and running away. One point at which escape was nearly impossible occurred when the trolley was traveling on the long trestle over the Woodcliff North Bergen Lake and the conductor would stop the trolley.

More commercial forms of thrill rides could be found at Palisade Amusement Park (now the site of Winston Towers Apartment Complex) in Cliffside Park and Columbia Amusement Park on Hudson Boulevard and 30ᵗʰ Street in North Bergen (now the site of a Shop Rite super market). Near Columbia Amusement Park was a night club called the "Top Hat" in which dinners and parties were hosted. In my younger years the opportunity to go to one of the parks with the chance to drive the "bumper" cars and a few of the high flying rides, was an accomplishment. As we got older the challenge of throwing a baseball at various objects for a prize drew our efforts.

At Journal Square in Jersey City, there were two large movie theaters. One was the Stanley Theater, known for the ornate and beautiful interior, which included an enormous crystal chandelier.

One of my friends made a regular Sunday trip to the Stanley. I made an extra effort to be playing with that friend on Sunday afternoon in hopes of getting an invitation to join them. We would take a bus ride from Union City to Jersey City for the movie and got candy or ice cream. I must admit that part of my motivation was avoiding my mother's regular trip to my father's grave, which created a little problem on my return.

During the 1930's at Christmas my mother would buy 5 or 10 gallons of pure alcohol to make cordials for the holidays. The alcohol was delivered in shining 5 gallon cans and then processed into the various flavored cordials, which were given as gifts to relatives and friends.

While writing this story on one occasion we had dinner at Ridgewood Country Club with Lisa, Joseph John, and Joseph Michael and the hostess for the evening was a young woman by the name of Eileen The name of that young lady brought back memories of my high school days, and part of my activities at the time. What, you may ask, does this have to do with Eileen?

Earlier in this story there is a pretty full explanation of my ice truck and Saturday Evening Post jobs taking place on Monday, Tuesday, Wednesday, Friday, and Saturday. Thursday and Sunday were not accounted for and that's where Eileen comes in. Eileen was a girl in my class, and daughter of Dr. Pagliughi who delivered me and my sister into the world.

And where does Thursday come into this story? I delivered ice to Dr. Pagliughi's house from 1929 to 1940 and milk from 1940 to 1943. In addition, every Thursday I had a job: cutting his very small back lawn and washing the windows (at 10 cents apiece). This might occupy maybe 3:30 to 4:30 in the afternoon. The doctor was usually home at that time for dinner.

While his wife was preparing dinner, he wanted to play ping pong in his basement. He and his daughter were aware that I belonged to a boys club (Hudson A.C.) where ping pong was the primary indoor sport, and that we competed with other local groups.

This is a pretty long story to get to the point of daughter Eileen. She was quite cute and was able to play the piano (now you see how my interest in the piano has been around

21

so long). The doctor only had limited time to play, so Eileen and I would fill in the time with ping pong and her playing the piano and me singing along.

I don't recall whether any proms were involved nor what happened after high school in this relationship. I also recall they had a summer home down at the Jersey shore and the doctor was able to buy a new Buick every year with a sticker price of about $700 less the trade-in value . . . Wealthy people!

CHAPTER TWO

1940 To 1943 – Milk Business and College

When I graduated in 1940 my brother got the idea of going into the milk business. We bought a 1929 Ford truck for 50 bucks, had it painted white and ordered two dozen bottles of milk (5 of them for our own family). While my brother continued to work as a toolmaker, I ran the milk business. At the end of 1940, we were able to buy a new 1941 Chevrolet truck with air conditioning and a radio, which was handy for Saturday night dates. A great improvement over the 1929 Ford!

When we started in business, milk was sold in bottles with a cream line on the top of the bottle. In selling to our customers, we would point out the fact that our milk had a deeper "cream" line than our competitors and therefore was a better value for the money. Diet was not a factor being considered.

In a few years, milk companies developed homogenization. This removed the cream line. So we had to advise our customers, that this was a better way of getting milk, as it was more easily digested—especially for the babies. Today, I wonder if it is possible to buy milk with the cream line and whether or not it would be argued that it would contain too much fat.

Through aggressive sales efforts by my brother and me, we increased our stock to about 300 quarts per day. We sold to small food stores and coffee shops. We delivered in the morning to the stores. At noon, we went to the shipyards in Weehawken to sell milk, soda, and sandwiches to the workers.

We even distributed half pints of milk in the factory where my brother worked. After the attack on Pearl Harbor, we were restricted from going around the plant. Our supplier, Hohneker Dairy, came up with a milk vending machine, with a glass top and slots through the top. This sold half-pint containers, retrieved with the use of a handle with a spring grip to place over the container. The customer would bring the container to the opening and the milk was released when the 15 cents was put into the machine. This was probably the first vending machine for milk.

We were able to place a machine near a tool station and have one of the factory employees refill the individual slots as needed from extra milk kept in a separate storage compartment in the machine. Of course, he got free milk for his efforts.

This proved so popular that by the time we went into the Army, the Dairy Company had a separate route for this type of business.

While it lasted it was a great way to make money while we were sleeping.

The delivery of milk evolved a great deal during my childhood. Originally, the milkman arrived in a horse-drawn carriage. At first, the wheels were of wood and you could hear the clatter of the wheels and the sound of the horses' hooves. The wheels were later covered with rubber tires but the sound of the hoofs remained. The animals were an effective partner to the milkman: the horses knew the actual route as well as the "driver" and would stop at the appropriate locations, without any input from the driver.

Despite my business success, I wanted to go to college. Before I could, however, I had to take additional math and science courses in high school. When I had started high school in 1936, my mother and sister had insisted I take a commercial course which did not fulfill the requirements for college. As I mentioned, even my brother Jerry who had graduated with a scholarship to Stevens Institute, had to work to help in support of the family. In the afternoons, after delivering milk, I completed my extra courses.

I was accepted for the September 1940 night division at St. Peter's College (then called Hudson College) in Jersey City. The classes were held four nights a week, usually 6:00 to 10:00 PM. I slept approximately 4 hours a day either 11:30 PM to 3:30 AM in the summer and 3:30 AM to 7:30 AM in the winter. In the winter, we could deliver earlier because the milk could remain outside the customer's house without spoiling.

In the spring of 1941, I went to my first college prom, held at the Knoll Country Club in Boonton, New Jersey.

My brother loaned me his new 1941 Plymouth car to take my date. I think her name was Pat Cosgrove, whose family were milk and previously ice customers of mine, which of course meant being sociable with the customer who happened to have young daughters.

Boonton is pretty far away from Jersey City, and many of the other students hired a bus which I followed. There was a long driveway up to the clubhouse and unfortunately the bus driver made a wrong turn on the driveway. He backed up and hit the front hood of my brother's new car before I could get out of the way.

I have forgotten the consequences that followed, but I know my mother had to intervene again, with my brother's anger. I can still remember the beautiful setting of the clubhouse, high on a hill overlooking the golf course. Many years later (probably in the 60's) I had the opportunity to play that course and have a bent left pinky finger as a result of an errant golf shot, (not unusual for me), into the bank of a stream just in front of the tee.

My problems, however, were about to get more serious and even my mother could not intervene to help me. Pearl Harbor brought on the necessity of black out curtains and shades and practice drills for possible bombing. It was hard to take this seriously at first: We thought we were safe because of the oceans dividing us from Japan and Germany.

Even before the United States joined the war, the country was on a war footing. Gasoline and food rationing were instituted. Plants that manufactured automobiles, trucks, furniture, clothing or food were converted to defense products. The Selective Service, better known as the draft, required all men, at first from age 21 to 35, then eventually from 18 to 45, to register for military service. When men were inducted into the army, women were called upon to go into the factories to do other essential work

The resulting lack of eligible students caused St. Peter's to close its night division in June 1942. I tried to transfer to John Marshall Law School in Jersey City which did not require an undergraduate degree. They would not give me credit for the year at Hudson College, so I applied to New York University where I was given full credit for my courses at Hudson. I enrolled for the night division with an accounting major. Classes were four nights a week but were made more difficult because I had to travel to Greenwich Village in New York City.

I continued in NYU until August 1943 when I was drafted into the Army. I requested a deferment. I was supporting my family, including my crippled brother and my brother, Jerry had gone into the Army in June of 1943. My appeal was rejected, and I was sent to Fort Dix for induction.

CHAPTER THREE

1943 To 1945—Army

Before I left home for the Army, Marie Puy, my brother's bed side teacher, gave me a card with a Prayer to St. Joseph. The original copy came from Ireland. We were told that all those who carried a copy of the prayer during the Civil and World Wars returned home without injury. Though not quite that lucky, I carried it throughout the war.

In September, I reported to Fort Dix for induction. After the usual interview, the Army ignored the fact that I was a college student and classified me a "truck driver". At the time I could not understand this classification but on reflection, that was how I earned my living. I was sent to Fort Knox in Kentucky for tank training.

Basic training lasted from September 1943 to January 1944. Bugle call at 5:30 AM roused us to police up the drill field (pick up any cigarette butts or other trash) whether needed or not, back to the barracks for breakfast and then back on the field for exercises.

Each day saw a different training program: how to dismantle and reassemble an M-1 rifle while blindfolded, how to shoot at a rifle range, how to fire hand guns and how to travel the hills of Kentucky with a compass in the middle of the night, both on foot and while driving an M-75 tank, to reach an assigned objective.

At Fort Knox, enlisted men bunked in an open barrack with the facilities for personal belongings being primarily in a foot locker at the foot of their bed. This proved to be quite interesting when the company Master Sergeant made an unscheduled barracks inspection to check the cleanliness of the bathrooms, the uniformity of the beds, and foot lockers or any hanging clothes that were permitted. I became friendly with a Platoon Sergeant by the name of Walter Todd. Our friendship gave me the privilege of sleeping in a private room at one end of the barrack.

Sergeant Todd also had access to a jeep for trips into Louisville and to the Women's' Army Corps or "WAC" barracks. During one of our trips, Todd became involved with a nice lady from Connecticut by the name of Eleanor. They eventually married in Connecticut and I was their Best Man.

Eleanor sends an annual letter, updating us on her family, her travels and other news of interest. She remained active in the WAC Veteran organization after the war and settled in New Orleans. She raised a family of five children and became a grandmother several times. As a source of income, she made dolls to be sold in the gift shops of New Orleans. One of her specialty dolls was named "Hattie" a happy Mammy type, who flipped over to reveal a Southern belle.

From Fort Knox, I was transferred in January 1944 to Fort Meade in Maryland, then later to Camp Shanks in Rockland County in New York. For the short time I spent at Fort Meade, I traveled home on the train into Newark N.J. on weekends. On one of the return trips, the train was so crowded, that I slept up on the luggage rack (Can you believe I was agile enough to do so?) I over-slept, past the Baltimore Station and ended up in Washington D.C. at 3:00 or 4:00 in the morning. Getting back to camp was not easy, which I believe combined "hitch hiking" and I think a short bus ride. I barely made the morning call. None of this excused me for the training scheduled for the day.

After a few weeks at Fort Meade we were transferred to Camp Shanks to await loading on the ship. The Rockland location was convenient for trips to Union City to pick up Italian cold cuts and cookies to bring back to camp. These trips generally were without permission. The threat of court martial made no difference when you knew you were being shipped overseas.

In February 1944, our company was assigned as a cleanup crew to the Queen Mary then making regular troop trips to England. This was a good assignment as we got C deck bunks (above water level), and could make friends with the kitchen crew. These crossings were escorted by battleships or smaller coast guard gunners, as the Germans had submarines prowling the North Atlantic. We landed in Southampton, England, which I believe was 5 days across the North Atlantic and transferred to Bristol, an Army staging area for the ultimate invasion to Europe. I was assigned to the Third Armored Division in the First Army under General Omar Bradley

The nearby towns were small and friendly. The English people, tired from the constant bombings, food rationing and other hardships, were happy to see American troops. All English citizens were involved in the war effort while suffering through the eerie screech and destruction of German bombs.

Obviously the influx of thousands of American soldiers had an effect on the economy as well as the social life. We were welcomed into their homes to share what provisions they had, and they were pleased with whatever food, even K rations or leftovers, that we could bring. Other than these home visits, the local pubs were the only recreational activity available.

Our training became more intense in anticipation of the actual invasion of France. In April and May, tension increased. In early June, the level of alert was heightened: we were prepared to move out in less than 24 hours.

On June 6, 1944, we knew the invasion was on. The air armada was awesome with highflying Bombers B-26, B-24, and fighter squadrons. The English Channel was choked with naval ships of all kinds. Our anxiety increased. We all knew the purpose we were here for and though we didn't want to die, we wanted to get it over with.

We were forced to wait until the 24th for the embarkation from Southampton and Weymouth (the name of the street in Wyckoff my daughter lives on). To the best of my recollection, we were loaded on LST (landing crafts) given a supply of D and K rations, plus PX supplies, motion sickness capsules and vomit bags. The equipment was well waterproofed and the channel lay ahead. We looked at each other—*I wonder how many of us will come back.*

I don't recall how long the crossing took but the channel was rough and the "accommodations" crammed with men and vehicles. The LST's were able to bring us close to shore but we were forced to walk in a couple feet of water. The sea was covered with the allied naval forces, from which fighter planes took off to reduce the potential of enemy aircraft.

We landed at Omaha Beach which had a 50 foot cliff, where the Germans had dug in monstrous artillery. Fortunately for us, the artillery had been silenced by earlier landings. (I will leave you to the horror of the beach as were shown in later movies which I have chosen not to see).

Our first sight of enemy troops was a procession of defeated troops with their hands over their head, straggling down the beach to board outgoing transports. In the other direction marched battalion after battalion of American soldiers, replacement for the infantry divisions up forward.

Assigned to areas a short distance from the beach, we spent our time preparing for combat operations. This area of France was farmland made up of separate areas, each about the size of a football field, used by the farmers for grazing and planting. The fields were separated by ancient hedgerows, which could contain 30 or 40-foot trees, high embankments and thick undergrowth.

All the highways and crossroads had been targeted by the enemy. By destroying one piece of equipment at that intersection, they could prevent any advancement on the roads. The alternative was to stay off the roads and cross through the hedgerows. This proved a nightmare for us.

To make our way, our company used one of the tanks outfitted with a bulldozer (we were lucky to have one of them) to break a hole in the embankment and undergrowth. If successful, we would proceed into the next field with other tanks following.

The Germans had a simple defense. They would leave one soldier on the other end of the field with an anti-tank gun and 50-caliber machine gun. He could destroy one or more tanks like sitting ducks.

We learned fast. The first tank that broke through had to spray the opposite hedge with machine gun fire, then to fire our 75 millimeter cannon at the site of the enemy's gun.

In some cases, we were able to call for P47 or P51 fighter planes to strafe the enemy placement. Still, this meant we were pursuing the enemy at the rate of 100 or 200 yards a day.

This was realized by high command and the plan changed to take to the country roads and bypass the fields.

By doing this, we were leaving individual German soldiers behind our lines or in position of snipers in the trees or in the ditches along the roads. Moreover, drainage ditches lined most roads, leaving places for potential ambushers to wait. While advancing on the roads was faster than the hedgerows, it was still quite slow. We could travel no faster than the infantry walking with us, although in some cases we could offer rides on the back of the tanks.

In one instance, while the infantry was walking alongside, a dug-in German soldier in a ditch fired a bazooka at my tank. My luck held: the shell hit the barrel of a rifle being carried by an infantryman. It was just enough to deflect it from the tank. I need not say how that enemy soldier ended up.

The end of July saw the famous St. Lo breakthrough when the Allied forces defeated the crack German Panzer divisions. We were fully on the offensive.

This is not to say the Germans had given up. They were retreating to reorganize their troops. They continued night bombings as our Air Force had taken control of the daytime air. We learned to distinguish the sound of enemy planes and gunfire from that of ours.

The breakthrough took place on July 26, 1944. 1800 heavy bombardment machines, 400 mediums, and close to 700 fighter-bombers flew over a relatively small area. There was an awe-inspiring, hypnotic quality about it, as Ernie Pyle an army correspondent, wrote.

> "The flight across the sky was slow and studied. I've never known a storm, or a machine, or any resolve of man that had about it the aura of such a ghastly relentlessness. I had the feeling that even if God appeared beseechingly before them in the sky, with palms outstretched to persuade them back, they would not have within them the power to turn their irresistible course. They stalked on, slowly, and with a dreadful pall of sound, as though they were seeing something at a greater distance and nothing existed between them. God, how we admired those men up there, and sickened for the ones that fell."

Mass in the field

I have a vivid memory of the sight and sound described. Our orders called for us to rev up the engines, take on a full load of gas and ammunition, and travel with support of the divisions of engineers, maintenance crews, artillery units, medical staffs and others. We were off. There was to be no stopping except for brief bits of sleep, grabbed an hour or so, in slit trenches dug under the tanks.

Gas and food supplies reached us whatever hour of the day or night they could catch us. Our gas supply was in 5 gallon cans which had to be dumped in the tank. I cannot recall the capacity of the tank, only to assure you it was a back breaking job.

The engineers were up front laying pontoon bridges over rivers too deep and too wide for us to cross. If a tank or other piece of equipment needed repair or replacement, the maintenance crews were there in relatively short order with another tank or half-track artillery truck.

More of our tanks were remodeled to include the bulldozer hedge cutting blades, and a revolving wheel attached to the front of the tank which could spin around to beat the ground in front and detonate any possible buried tank—destroying grenades.

We had direct communication with a fighter air group, through air personnel riding in one of our forward tanks. If crossing an open field, we might draw enemy artillery fire from a hill in front of us. If we were unable to disable it with our artillery, we could call on a couple P47 or P51 to strafe the enemy area. The memory of those many encounters caused me to be apprehensive when I came home and a high hill was off in the distance.

In another instance I was the lead tank in a convoy traveling down the road, and we drew fire from a German Panzer with 88 mm cannons heading in our direction. The first shell was off to one side. The second was over our head and off to the other side.

We returned our 75 mil cannon fire but without success and the German tank continued toward us. Their next shell would have been on target, and our end. My tank commander called for the gun loader to fire a phosphorus shell, which fortunately hit the front of the German tank and burned a hole thru its turret, causing a fire and the soldiers obviously to dismount.

I remember open fields, small farm towns where we rumbled our tanks and equipment through the narrow streets, taking out parts of buildings as we maneuvered. In some of the towns, we were greeted by the French people with flags and banners. In some cases, we witnessed French men or women—believed to be Nazi collaborators—dragged through the street with shaven heads and torn clothing. If a German artillery horse were shot down, it was not unusual to see the Frenchmen gather to cut up the carcass for food.

I was involved in the actual combat until wounded in November 1944. We had reached the first objective of that advance, which was a little farm town with one cross road. Our tanks were set up to protect this cross road while other forces would reach their objective some miles east or west of where we were.

The turret of the 75 mm gun would be aimed down the side road (we'll say facing east) to encounter any enemy forces which may come down the road, though the front of the tank would be facing down the other way. (We'll say facing north.) While in this position it was not unusual for us to open our hatches and sit up in our seats with at least our heads out of the tank for some fresh air.

Unfortunately some enemy artillery fire hit the turret of my gun which was less than a foot from where my head was up out of the tank. The shrapnel damaged the turret and cut my cloth hat. We were told to go back to our reserves and get another tank or try and have this repaired. Up to this time I lost a total of 4 tanks.

MJF-in-Hospital

MJF-in Paris

While going back it became evident that the shell affected my hearing as I could not hear the tank commander's instructions while driving "buttoned up". This determination had the medics decide I should return to the field hospital, to see the extent of my injury, then a Paris hospital and finally back to London. Why I was taken off the front lines, to this day I do not know: my injury consisted of a punctured ear drum, which affected my hearing to some degree. This was a very minor injury considering the more serious condition of other soldiers.

Upon release from the hospital, I was fortunate to be assigned to the Message Center in Eisenhower Headquarters known as SHAEF [Supreme Headquarters Allied Expedition Forces], which at that time was located in the Palace of Versailles. This was certainly a great assignment—far from the front lines, with a short trip to Paris and camaraderie of British troops also assigned to this Headquarters. One of the buildings was an Officer's Club which I was able to visit quite frequently as a friend of British Sergeants who were allowed into the club and were friendlier than the U.S. officers.

While at Versailles, I had the occasion to meet a high school friend of mine in an adjoining company. This was unusual in and of itself but of more immediate interest: this friend was the Sergeant in charge of the kitchen. His name was Harold Walling and he was married to his high school sweetheart, Ruth. I was reminded of Harold today (September 2002) while talking to Joe D'Elia's sister Helen who is a neighbor of Ruth. Reminded of my wartime friend, I called Ruth.

We had kept in touch after the war: I had prepared their wills and handled the closing of their house. Ruth told me that Harold had died of colon cancer several years ago. She and her daughter continue to live in the two-family house I handled for them.

It is evident that General Eisenhower knew how to pick out locations for their function. It was a major city with fine accommodations. This Headquarters was later moved to Frankfort, Germany to occupy the extensive complex known as the I G Farben headquarters. The war ended in Europe in April 1945. Being in the message center, I got early notice of the announcement to the world. I remained with Headquarters through the surrender of Japan in August 1945, and then was processed for discharge to Belgium for shipping home.

My orders were issued about December 1, 1945. Unfortunately, I damaged a tooth while eating what turned out to be a horse steak. Necessary dental work caused an interruption in the processing.

The paperwork was finally finished about the 15th of December. I was anxious to be home for Christmas, which unfortunately didn't happen. The freighter, to which I was assigned, with 20 other soldiers and 20 crew members, had a 20-day trip skirting storms in the Atlantic. We reached New York about the 3rd of January 1946.

Outwardly unchanged, I did notice some differences in myself when I returned from the war. For instance, I found a great deal of difficulty if someone said "they needed" something. I had learned how little we actually *need* to exist, if not to live. We had K and D rations, which were nutritious enough (or so they told us). Our primary liquid was water. Utensils were cleaned by rubbing them in the dirt. Shaving was out of a helmet of water, washing was pretty rare and toilet facilities consisted of digging a hole in the ground and covering it over. You can imagine our satisfaction and enjoyment when we were back from the frontline, in the rear where engineers set up outhouses and portable showers, and the kitchen company caught up to us for a hot meal and hot coffee.

CHAPTER FOUR

1945 To 1947 – Florida Trip With Army Buddies, NYU Fraternity, And Meeting Grace

The last segment had me returning to the US in January 1946. I was discharged that month and followed up on a plan I had made with a couple of Army buddies for a trip to Florida.

It was the first time for me, and I believe the other two, who were from the Bronx. Never did I think that, in later years, I would be making many more trips to that state.

After driving a couple of days – this was before Interstate 95 was built—we reached our destination in Miami Beach, a hotel on Collins Avenue and, I think, 39th Street. Being adventurous characters after the war experience, we decided to go to Cuba to experience the night life.

While there, we made friends with an older retired builder (maybe in his fifties) from Long Island, who was on his honeymoon with his younger wife. While in Cuba, he met a couple of old cronies from New York who, I think, were "on the lam" from U.S. authorities. In any event, he was having a great time with them and wasn't anxious to go home. At the request of his new wife, we convinced him to get on the plane back.

The next time I heard from him, he had discovered my home address in Union City and visited with some imported wine. I wasn't interested in the wine, but I did think about his offer to join him to Florida in a construction business. I declined the offer (can I speculate on the consequences of that decision?). I wanted to return to NYU for completion of my accounting degree. He tried again, several times after but to no avail.

While in Florida, we also met a couple who owned extensive real estate in Hudson County near where I lived. I had known of the family. To my surprise, on my return to Union City, I received a call from the wife, inviting me and my Army buddies to Sunday dinner at their home in Fort Lee. Without any expectation, except of a free meal, we accepted.

Their house was a gated mansion overlooking the Hudson River and New York on the cliffs in Fort Lee just north of the George Washington Bridge. We sat down for dinner in a very large dining room with the parents on each end of the table, the three of us on one side and their three daughters on the other. Another young couple sat opposite each other.

I recall the daughters were between 18 and 22. Two attended NYU. During dinner, their mother suggested (none too subtly) that their daughters were available for dating and possibly marriage. In addition, they expounded on the extent of their real estate business and their need for some nice young men to help out. Whatever that might have led to, I'm glad it didn't happen. I would have missed meeting the beautiful girl I married.

In returning to NYU, I joined thousands of other GI's. The GI bill provided the tuition cost. For living money, I worked in the mailroom of the New York Times on Friday and Saturday.

I got the job and its good pay through the efforts of my cousin Nicky Fruschi, whose friend was the Union shop steward.

I was also invited to join a fraternity. I chose Delta Sigma Pi, considered a "commercial" fraternity, with impressive alumni who would be valuable after graduation for contacts.

Delta Sigma Pi had a fraternity house on McDougal Street about three blocks from school. I met many guys who would become long-time friends. Among them was Ted Boutis, who may have been the pledge master along with Cliff Milton. Rodney Stahl was another member. I pledged with Vince Schuster. Later members of the fraternity included Paul Lee and Jack Buitine.

Though college was years ago, many of us continue to keep in contact. Ted Boutis married a girl named Jane. They adopted three children: Ted (my godson), Pricilla and Elizabeth.

Cliff Milton (who we thought was going to be a bachelor) married a sorority girl named Terry. They bought a house in Cresskill (where another fraternity brother Rodney Stahl lived) and raised a family of one son and three daughters. Cliff was in advertising and marketing for many years with the Carrier Air Conditioning Company. I have handled the sale and purchase of homes for them. Terry died, but Cliff and I still communicate.

Paul Lee became the first National sales manager for the Volkswagen Company in the 60's, but moved from the area and we lost track of him.

Vinnie Schuster and his wife Elaine had two children: Steven, a lawyer in Bergen County, and Karen, a teacher for special education children. After Elaine died, Vince remarried and moved to Florida.

Rodney Stahl helped me get my Borough Attorney position in Cresskill, where he was living with his wife, a nurse.

Through the fraternity, I was elected to the Student Council, which gave me the opportunity to get tickets to Madison Square Garden for NYU championship basketball games and free tickets to dinners and dances held by the school.

All of this is secondary to the most important single event of my life.

In addition to the fraternity, I had joined the Catholic Newman Club, which had a club room in the basement of one of the brownstones surrounding Washington Square in Greenwich Village. One afternoon, I walked into the club and saw a very nice young lady dressed in a red suit sitting next to a piano. There was a Perry Como (my competition) record playing. I asked her to dance and the rest is history (want to guess who?).

Fraternity House

In the Spring of 1946, the school held a formal dinner and dance at the Hotel Pierre. I decided to ask Grace if she wanted to go (give the kid a break, I thought). Of course, I could not conceive of any reason she wouldn't jump at the opportunity. To my surprise, she said she would have to think about it, as her brothers were coming home from Massachusetts that weekend. I couldn't believe this would have any priority over my invitation, but I learned quickly the importance of family to Grace. Fortunately she agreed to come with me.

When I went to pick her up in Queens, her mother, realizing that on my long trip from Jersey; I might have forgotten to visit a florist; had prepared a beautiful white camellia corsage from her green house.

Around this time, Grace and I began to enjoy Broadway shows. Her brother John and his wife Mary were visiting the Deliso family home in Ozone Park. John decided on the spur of the moment to see a Broadway show. He was able to get four tickets to the hit show of the time, *Brigadoon*. Because of this last minute planning, all he could get were four seats in the last row of the balcony. The show was memorable: first a Broadway show with my girl friend and spending time with one of her brothers.

It was not too many years later when my brother Jerry and I embarked on a regular program of theater going. The shows we saw included *The Sound Of Music*, *Gentlemen Prefer Blondes*, *Oklahoma*, *My Fair Lady*, *South Pacific*, *The King and I*, *Fiorello*, *Flower Drum Song*, *Camelot*, *The Wizard of Oz*, and many more I can't recall. The music from these shows continues to provide enjoyment.

In recent years, we've continued the practice. Ridgewood Country Club has trips to Broadway with dinner at the club, a bus to the theater and a return trip to the club for dessert. In addition, Grace and a small group of ladies go to a Wednesday lunch and matinee a few times a year.

Back to my college years: In summer, 1946, my friends decided to have a beach party at Jones Beach. Again, I asked Grace. The girls prepared lunches for their beaus. When it came time to eat, I noticed the lunches prepared by the other girls had mundane American bread sandwiches. Grace, however, had made old-fashioned Italian hero sandwiches. I knew then, this was the girl for me!

After a year or more of making the extended subway and bus trips to Queens, in November 1947 I suggested (it is usually called proposing) that we get married. I popped the question in Washington Square Park in Greenwich Village. We formalized our engagement with the exchange of rings at Midnight Mass at St. Rocco's Church in Union City, Christmas 1947

As Grace reminds me, when she agreed to become engaged, she was taking a real gamble. Here she was, a nice Italian girl from a respectable family of Ozone Park, New York, with no end of available returning GI's and other long time friends in the area.

Now this wise guy from New Jersey makes a move. Of course, he was smart enough to use the Newman Catholic Club at NYU as the initial location for the move. She was taking courses for a Master's degree while teaching in a Brooklyn High School. In making the decision to marry me, she was prepared to give up her career and deprive future generations of New York City school children of her talents, even though she did continue to work for a while after we got married.

CHAPTER FIVE

1947 To 1950 – Law School, Engagement, Marriage

Having reached this important stage of our relationship, the natural follow-up was to talk about the marriage date. As is not uncommon, we were all over the board on the date. When will we have enough money for it? What are our commitments of family or education and professional [to wit: a paying job]?

As I mentioned, my cousin Nicky Fruschi, who worked in the mail room of the New York Times, was able to get me a part time job, which paid well while I finished undergraduate and law school.

During this same time, I developed an accounting business, servicing many small retail businesses like pizza shops, dress factories, embroidery shops, taverns and real estate owners. I also helped landlords and tenants with rent control problems.

When I returned to NYU in 1946, I had accumulated 25 to 30 credits of the 120 or 128 required. I took the maximum credits allowed (16 or 18 per term). I took both summer sessions and had the required credits by September 1947.

I applied to NYU Law School and was fortunate to be accepted, considering there were thousands of GI's applying and I did not have very high grades. The retiring Dean of the Law School, Arthur Vanderbilt, a prominent New Jersey Republican politician believed good grades were not the only or even the best criteria for admission to law school. A lawyer must also be able to relate to public needs. He later became the Chief Justice of the New Jersey Supreme Court following a Constitutional Convention restructuring the entire court system.

For Dean Vanderbilt, the fact that I was on the Student Council all of my college years and had good references from the School of Commerce Dean was the deciding factors. Just being admitted, however, was no guarantee of becoming an attorney. 200 students were admitted with the clear understanding only half would be able to reach the second year. Somehow, I managed to reach that level, despite my fledging accounting practice, job at the *Times*, and courting Grace.

In 1947, the law school was in the old main school building, in Washington Square. After my graduation in 1950, a new law school was built on the Square, displacing (among other buildings) the fraternity house of Delta Sigma Pi.

The fraternity life continued to be the foundation of my social life and also provided my first important accounting client, the Florence Shop in Bergenfield, New Jersey. The Florence Shop was owned by Florence Eberhardt, the aunt of my fraternity brother Vince Schuster.

After we decided to get married, we started to consider where we would live. It was pretty much understood that our home would be New Jersey. That was where I had my limited practice and Grace could still travel to New York to teach. The next important question was the type of housing—an apartment or a house. The latter seemed to be out of the question until Grace revealed she had saved about $2,000 which could be used as a down payment.

With Grace's teaching, her nest egg and my two part-time jobs in hand, we contacted real estate brokers. The GI Bill of Rights provided a Veterans' Administration mortgage at 4 ½ percent. We probably had income of only about $5,000 a year, but we looked at houses as high as $19,000. Not really sure we could manage, yet confident and optimistic, we pushed on.

This search created another milestone in our life when Fourman Real Estate found a house for us in Bergenfield on Highgate Terrace. The asking price was $13,500. The broker suggested we offer $10,000. We bought the house for $11,200. With Grace's $2,000, a $500 loan from my cousin Nicky and a $9,200 GI mortgage, I believe the monthly payment was $72 including interest, principal and taxes.

As little as that may seem, it required very careful budgeting. There were no movies or eating out. Even though both of us had grown up using butter, 48 cents a pound, we convinced ourselves that margarine was better for us at 27 cents a pound. The house closing took place in April 1949.

We took title in my name alone, because we would not be married until July. Grace's security in this arrangement was her five brothers who could protect her interest if necessary.

The real estate broker involved was Jud Toomey. Later, Jud formed a mortgage business and asked me to do some accounting work for him. After I passed the Bar, I did some legal work for his company.

Between the closing in April and the wedding in July, we redecorated this cute house. It was two stories high with two bedrooms and a bath on the second floor, a living room, dining room and kitchen on the first floor, and a screened-in back porch. We agreed that Grace would eat in the kitchen while I ate in the dining room. The kitchen and dining room were so small, well, maybe not that small: to save space, I installed a drop leaf table in the doorway which would be pulled up when we ate.

Our furniture consisted of a bedroom set, a three-piece living room set, dining room table and four chairs purchased from a Worcester Massachusetts factory in a building owned by Grace's brothers. The second bedroom was furnished with a three piece maple set – an arm chair, rocking chair and couch, which could be opened to use as a bed – given to us as a wedding gift from Grace's brother Mike and his wife Frances. Today in 2006, the chairs are still being used by one of our daughters. Her brother John and his wife Mary gave us a very nice meat carving set. The redecorating turned out beautifully.

The wedding was at The Nativity of the Blessed Virgin on July 23, 1949 in Ozone Park, N.Y. The reception took place in the back hall of a tavern in Ozone Park. Because of our tight budget, only our immediate families attended.

The most important part of the day after the ceremony was carrying Grace (yes, she was that light) over the threshold of our own house.

For our honeymoon, we had our new car (a 1949 Plymouth bought for $750 through Grace's brother John's contact in Worcester) and planned a 2-week honeymoon to New England and Canada.

We left on the afternoon of the 24th and drove to somewhere in Connecticut. From there, we drove to Cape Cod heading to Provincetown. The weather turned rainy and we decided to continue to New Hampshire, finding a small motel complex of six or seven cabins on the side of a hill, overlooking open fields. It was a very nice setting.

We drove to Canada and ended up in a small motel with a tavern connected—the best we could afford. It was late, and we had made no advance reservations for this trip.

We were obviously young and "adventurous". We drove to St. Anne de Beaupré, east of Quebec, and then stayed at the magnificent hotel Chateau-Frontenac. From there, we headed west to Ottawa, capital of Canada and then onto Toronto. We were impressed with the extensive business community underground.

Our next objective was the "Honeymoon Capital of the World"—Niagara Falls. They really are spectacular to see. In an attempt to photograph them at night, I placed our little inexpensive camera on the roof of the car and placed my wallet of travel checks under the lens to take a time-exposed picture. Having done so, we returned to the hotel about 9:00 when I realized I didn't have the travel checks. We went back immediately with no success. We returned very early the next morning only to learn that the streets were washed and no checks found.

American Express ads today tout how easy it is to replace the lost checks. I can only say that in 1949, it was not that easy. We had to conserve our cash on the way home. We had enough to stop at Howe Caverns (also spectacular) and headed home with a total of ten, rather than 14 day vacation. But I can assure you, the return to our beautiful Highgate Terrace home was as good as any part of the trip. Several weeks later American Express reimbursed us the lost checks.

Grace continued teaching in Brooklyn, which required her to be up at 5:30 AM to get a bus, then a subway to be at school by 8:00 AM. She asked to be transferred closer to

New Jersey. The Board of Education was glad to assign her to East Harlem at 102nd Street and First Avenue.

Our plans for me to finish school, be admitted to the New Jersey bar and have a "legitimate" job were faltering. School was a three-year program, and I hoped to be finished by June 1950. Unfortunately, I flunked a Future Interests (an arcane real estate course) which I took in the summer of 1950. I graduated with the class of 1951.

After law school, I had to clerk with a lawyer for at least nine months before I could take the bar examinations. While doing that in Judge Cozzi's office, I was able to use my accounting knowledge and handle rent control cases for landlords and tenants.

But that's getting ahead of the story. In July 1949, we were married and owned a house, with Grace teaching and the main support of the family. It was our understanding that she would continue until I was able to fulfill my responsibility to support my wife.

For our understanding to work, we had to stick to the plan. When you are married to a beautiful lady and are in love, however, God can have plans of His own, as with the birth of Virginia (named after Grace's mother) on June 8, 1950. Our joy with our first daughter cannot be described. Until February, Grace still traveled to East Harlem at 5:30 each morning so we could pay the mortgage, taxes and food bills.

My sister Virginia helped Grace and me in preparation for our first child. My cousin, Dr. Colonna, was our family doctor. His office was in West New York, a 20 minute drive from Bergenfield. He had privileges at St. Mary's Hospital in Hoboken, where all our children were born.

I took the New Jersey bar examination in February, June and (finally successful) in October 1951. I now had the license to unshackle my hands to earn a living. In raising our family, Grace often had to function with the limited income I was able to provide. All of our meals were prepared by Grace and little or no outside restaurants.

Our first daughter Virginia was born in 1950, Donna in 1953, and Lisa in 1956. Of course, for Grace, they didn't compare to taking on the real headache, Michael J. in 1949.

We have all benefited from Grace's love and sacrifice. She has been the stalwart guidance of our daughters, of whom we are extremely proud. She taught them the real values of life and the joy and problems of marriage and children. Their husbands are also beneficiaries of Grace's wisdom.

I unhesitatingly, and have many times publicly stated, that the best thing I ever did was marry my wife. She has been an uncomplaining supporter in whatever endeavor I chose. I can assure you some of them caused an extra tightening of the belt. Any accomplishments I may have achieved would not have been possible without her at my side—and maybe sometime in front of me.

Our children attended Queen of Peace elementary school. When the time came for high school, Virginia was in the first class of the newly established archdiocesan school, Paramus Catholic. Donna chose another of the new established archdiocesan schools, Immaculate Heart Academy in Washington Township. Lisa chose to follow Donna and attend Immaculate Heart Academy as well. At the that point we had one daughter already in college at Elizabeth Seton Junior College in Yonkers, N.Y., and two daughters in private parochial high schools. The required uniforms kept clothing bills to a minimum and dresses for the holidays were often made by Grace.

I could now say I had a legitimate job with a regular salary of $125 per week to supplement my accounting and tax preparation fees. The work succeeded to the point that I got a raise to $150 per week. Grace's prudence again came forward. She said we have been "living" on the previous salary so we should save the rest. It enabled us to buy a $25 U.S. savings bond [I think for $18] each week, which later was used for the purchase of our Maywood house.

CHAPTER SIX

1950 To 1958—Mortgage Company

Shortly after passing the bar, I received a call from Jud Toomey, the real estate agent in the purchase of our first house. He asked me to assist with some accounting work in the mortgage business he was opening in Hackensack. I agreed and mentioned that I had just passed the bar and was available to do legal work as well.

The added responsibility of a lawyer closing real estate deals involved hundreds of thousands of dollars of construction mortgages for the enormous developments taking place in Bergen County. The irony of this, you will recall, is that I had flunked the Future Interest course involving real-estate.

My activity with Toomey-Fountain Mortgage had me closing titles on 5 or 6 house deals a day with GI and FHA mortgages. The population of Bergen County was 539,139 in 1950 and has grown to 897,569 in 2003.

Working with Jud involved deals for individual houses as well as large tracts of homes, in Bergen County, New Jersey A few of the builders were John Ingannamorte, Frank Melehan, and Frank Joy, the Wells brothers, Cal Sergent, Gary Berman, and many other smaller builders.

At the time, many open parcels still existed in Paramus, New Milford, Closter, Demarest and Hillsdale, and certainly in the Northwest and Northeast portions of Bergen County

Paramus's corn fields and fruit farms went quickly, followed by the celery farms. In the fifties, came the shopping centers, with Bergen Mall first in 1957 or 1958, followed by Garden State Plaza in 1960, Lord and Taylor's Fashion Center in Ridgewood, Paramus Park with Sears Roebuck and Abraham & Strauss (later purchased by Macy's) as anchor stores, the Route 4 Multiple complex movies, and Alexander's (replaced in 2003 by IKEA).

The same period brought the large garden apartments in New Milford and Fair Lawn, and high rise apartments in Fort Lee, Hackensack and Cliffside Park. Ingannamorte bought the Holy Angels Academy in Fort Lee and built the Mediterranean Towers Apartments on its site. In Cliffside Park, the Horizon Apartment complex was built on the land of Palisades Amusement Park, which had been widely known for its salt water pool and professional entertainment.

When I was with Toomey-Fountain Mortgage Company in 1952, mortgage financing required a line of credit which was secured by mortgages on real estate. This was called "warehousing", with the mortgage held by a warehousing bank until the VA and FHA paper was completed and the mortgage was assigned to the permanent lender.

John Joel was counsel to a warehousing bank at that time known as Commonwealth Trust in Union City. This was only one of such banks, but one of the more active with Toomey-Fountain, because of John's longstanding relationship with Jud Toomey.

Sometime in the 1970's, John's law firm closed. By chance, about that time, I met John in the Paramus Park food area. I suggested he could come into my office without cost and carry out whatever business he had. He was extremely happy and arranged for his sister Anne to come from Jersey City where she lived (in the same house for 50 years) to continue as his secretary (which she was from 1931 when he first passed the bar).

A close relationship developed. John and Anne were with me until John died in May 20, 1991 and Anne died August 6, 1999.

Frank Melehan was one of my first clients with the Toomey-Fountain Mortgage Co. At the time, he was a full time fireman in Teaneck, working alternate 24-hour shifts. On his days off, he started to build a "spec" house and on his days in the firehouse, various sub-contractors would work on the house.

Next to the firehouse on Teaneck Road, Fourman Real Estate had an office (you may recall this was the agency which handled my first house).

The agency had its original office on 48th Street in Union City and I knew them prior to coming to Bergen County. Pete Quilla and Harry Moore were owners of the agency. They met Melehan and decided to set up a venture: Fourman would find a vacant lot, Melehan would build a house and Fourman would find the buyers. To say the least, you can see the profits for Fourman.

Alexander Summer was another large real estate broker in Teaneck and Bergen County. They offered Melehan an opportunity to build a development in Closter. Because of the time requirements, the officials of Teaneck told Frank he had to make up his mind either remain a fireman—with its weekly salary, pension and security—or a builder—with the possibility of considerable profit.

At this time, we know the answer: he went on to build many other developments, both commercial properties like the Benjamin Moore Headquarters, the A&P Headquarters, Lehn & Fink in Montvale, and many other homes, including in the higher price market in Saddle River.

He and his wife Pat raised 9 children, all of whom went to private schools then advanced to college and graduate degrees. Early in the family growth, he built a log house at Greenwood Lake. Traveling every day to Bergen County in the winter started to take a toll.

Through a lawyer by the name of Chick Harrison, who was also a land developer, Frank bought a 2-acre lot on Fox Hedge Road in Saddle River to build a considerably larger house to accommodate the family. I put this detail in the story as I was representing Frank in these deals. He offered me a lot in Saddle River at very reasonable price (a little bartering system to be involved). Grace, however, was not anxious to join Pat Melehan driving children back and forth to school and after school programs. In Maywood, our children rode the bus to school. I said no thank you.

Many years later, he again offered us a lot. We had enough interest to hire an architect and drew up plans for what was to be our dream house. As usual, we had "Champagne taste with beer pockets" and the college years were upon us.

Frank entered the Florida market building extensive housing complexes and high-rise buildings. He again offered us a deal in Jupiter, which we were not up to yet. We did ultimately buy an apartment on the west side of the Intercoastal Waterway in Jupiter. Market conditions changed and we sold it before moving in. This started to pique our interest in Florida and we looked at several of his other projects in that area of Florida.

The rest of the Melehan house story is that we are now living in Spring Meadow complex built by him in Wyckoff. Melehan remains a good friend, sponsoring me for membership in Ridgewood Country Club in 1973, which Grace and I have enjoyed immensely.

In the 1950's, I met Frank Joy, a builder with his father in Bergenfield, New Milford and Tenafly. His father retired and Frank continued with a corporation known as Deerfield Homes. He built homes in a higher price range ($75,000 to $100,000) in Fair Lawn and Oradell. One of his luxury projects was the Blauvelt Estates in Oradell with prices in the $150,000 plus range. He offered me the garden lot behind the Blauvelt mansion but again we couldn't make up our mind to move.

One of his last projects was in Ridgewood on Murray Hill Drive. It consisted of seven lots and a mansion house in which he lived. The lots were priced from $400,000 to $700,000, and the houses exceeded the million-dollar mark.

One other early client was the Ingannamorte family. They built homes and garden apartments in Fair Lawn, Dumont, New Milford, a small shopping plaza in Cresskill and the Mediterranean Towers apartments in Fort Lee. John Ingannamorte was the most active member of the operation and we developed a close relationship.

When I was setting up the Bergen Bank of Commerce, John and his brother Mike became incorporators. John later became involved in the Republican Party as a financial supporter and later as the County Chairman.

It was through his effort that I became the Attorney for the Board of Freeholders in 1986, when the new charter form of government was approved. I served until December 2000 when the Democrats became the majority party on the Freeholders.

While serving the Freeholders, John and I were close confidants and friends. I had the pleasure and honor to be invited to the weddings of his daughter, Linda and son, John, which needless to say were elaborate and outstanding. Our friendship continues here as well as in Florida.

I first met Ed Dresher in 1952 when I moved my law office to 166 Main Street in Hackensack, which was owned by his father. This move was required by the County Ethics committee to separate from the mortgage company, referred to earlier. Ed had an office stationery store in the same building that had a section for house gifts. They were in the process of closing out that section, which resulted in our getting some items in our young married life.

Ed was an avid golf fan. Over the years, he nurtured many young golf professionals. He had given them some office equipment when they were setting up at a country club and even had a second bedroom for their use in his Florida home. Some pros remained friends when they went on to major pro status. One example, Bruce Fleischer, participated in the PGA Senior Open at Ridgewood Country Club in 2001. Ed and I have remained friends and nearly have daily telephone contact along with occasional lunches.

In the 70's, his son-in-law, Steve Specter, became one of my law partners. Steve became borough attorney in East Paterson, (now Elmwood Park) and later County Counsel for a period of time.

These individuals have remained relatively close friends to this day.

By the year 1955, with our second child Donna (born in May 1953) and the third, Lisa, to be born in January 1956, it became clear our cute little house in Bergenfield was too small.

Through the mortgage business, I met a builder by the name of Manfredi who had built a house in Maywood. He was having marital troubles, and neither he nor his wife could agree on a buyer. My good fortune came forward again and they agreed to sell it to us (notice I said *us*: Grace's ownership interest had been duly recorded on the Bergenfield house after we were married). The purchase price, I believe, was $32,000.

With the equity of the Bergenfield house now about $8,000 over the mortgage, our savings bonds and another GI mortgage of about $22,000, we bought 69 Locust Drive, Maywood, New Jersey. This house had about 2700 square feet—at least 2½ times larger than Bergenfield. This closing took place in November 1955 and the added bedroom space was ready for the third blessing, Lisa's arrival, in January 1956.

Before I would buy the house, it was necessary to have complete agreement from Grace. I asked her to tell me not what she liked about the house, but rather what she didn't like, as I knew that's what I would forever hear. She didn't want the laundry machines in the basement.

The original plan of the house included an attached garage with two or three steps down from the kitchen. When the house was being built, Manfredi found the grade of land required a lot of fill to raise the garage to the kitchen level. Instead, he put the garage on the lower level. In doing so, the actual garage would be 12 to 13 feet lower than the foundation of the house. This left an empty open space. He then decided to add a room above the one-car garage and an extra stair case.

After a little consideration, I decided to eliminate the extra staircase, install a floor over the same space, and use the extra space in the cellar as a second garage by installing two steel beams front and back and side-to-side to support the garage and house. This gave Grace a laundry room between the kitchen and the family room above the garage.

The style of the house was called a two-story expanded ranch. It had two bedrooms and a full bath on the second floor and a master bedroom with full bath, on the first floor. Also on the first floor were a 27 by 15 ½ foot living room and a 15½-foot square dining room. The kitchen was 23½ feet by 13 feet. Off the living room was a 14-foot square wood paneled study. The room over the garage on the other side of the house was 14 feet wide by 20 feet long. Off the kitchen, were a powder room and a door to the backyard. Later, we added a large deck off the kitchen and the dining room.

We moved into the house in November 1955 and short time after it became cold enough to put the heat on. One night, we heard a clicking noise and were concerned there were mice running around the house. We called the exterminator and he did his job. He found no problem, but the noise continued. With further investigation, we learned it was the hot water heating system, with which we were not familiar because the Bergenfield house had a hot air system.

Our Maywood home had several unique features, one of which was the 1200 square foot basement with a 9-foot ceiling and an entrance from the driveway. The basement permitted me to enjoy ping pong. I set up two tables and hung large commercial-type fluorescent lamps over each of them. On one side of the basement was a 38-foot area to play, permitting plenty of backspace for the game. The other side was a slight bit smaller, with about 25 feet depth.

The floor activity threw up so much cement dust that we needed a tile floor. Grace and I did a major part of the labor, which included heating the tiles in a toaster oven before pressing them in the black paste. This basement also provided a very nice indoor play area for the girls to learn to roller skate and ride bicycles

We organized a ping pong team of about 10 men and arranged games with other towns. We played once a week, practicing and socializing on other nights. Grace baked us many different cakes which proved a consistent hit even if our games were not.

Many of the men were involved in local business, professions and politics. Probably the best player was Len Rubin who owned and published the local newspaper, *Our Town*. Len was involved in many community activities including the Easter Seals drive, the blood bank drives, and the annual golf tournament.

The basement also became a place for us to take dancing lessons with friends from the Hackensack UNICO group. Grace prompted the lessons by declaring, if I was going to UNICO and political functions, she wasn't going to sit around while I "worked the crowd".

Among my friends in Maywood politics were Chet Eccleston and John Stuert – both had served as mayor – and George Croonquest, a councilman, who advanced as a stock broker to become a director of Janney-Montgomery Scott.

When we moved into Maywood in November 1955, the Bergen Mall Shopping center was being proposed in Paramus with a small portion of it in Maywood. The boundary of Maywood and Paramus was at the rear of our property. I attended council meetings about the Mall in Maywood and Paramus.

Early on, some political people in Maywood approached me to run for local office. I declined the offer, but it opened a door into the Republican Organization. I became a County Committeeman, President of the Maywood Republican Club and the Maywood Borough Attorney. Later, I was selected as a candidate for the New Jersey Assembly by the County Republican organization.

CHAPTER SEVEN

Golf And Rivervale Country Club

I started to play golf with my brother Jerry; a friend of his, "Ginger" Schwartz and Frank Melehan, who was probably my first builder client in 1952 or 1953. We played at the Saddle River Public course in Paramus on Sunday mornings at about 7:00. Ginger was the only one who didn't go to church, so he would go to the course at 6:00 and put our golf bags on line. The rest of us made 5:45 AM Mass at Holy Trinity church in Hackensack (across the street from my present office).

We would stop at a diner on Route 4 for a fast breakfast and get to the course about seven. We finished by the latest 11:30, going home for lunch and family jobs like cutting the lawn. Many afternoons, I would fill the car with the family to explore the roads of northern Bergen and Rockland County. I later put a compass on the dashboard (they now have them built in) to avoid getting lost completely.

Often, a stop was made at Tice Farms (now gone) for donuts, ice cream, apples and peaches. In August and September, we bought bushels of peaches for Grace to preserve for my private stock. If a friend came to visit us during the winter, I might even send them home with a jar of my treasure.

In the late 50's, I started to play golf with my fraternity brothers at the River Vale Country Club owned by Nick Porreca.

Sometime later (probably in 1959 or so), I had entered into the Maywood "Our Town" golf tournament, run by Len Rubin. Among the other players was Father Ed Kearney, a priest in our local Catholic Church. Father Kearney suggested that some of us should try to play golf together more than once per year. Based on that suggestion, we set up a foursome of Father Kearney, Ed Duflocq, Len Rubin and me. I classified this as a group of four major religions: a Catholic Priest (Father Kearney), a Jewish newspaper man (Len Rubin), a Protestant personnel manager (Ed Duflocq), and an Italian, which I made a new religion. We played five or six games per year, for about the next 19 years. We played about 100 or 101 different course in New Jersey, New York, Connecticut, Pennsylvania and Massachusetts. Most times we played private courses like Baltustrol in New Jersey and Merion Country Club in Pennsylvania, The Country Club in Massachusetts, the National Country Club in Long Island and, of course, Ridgewood Country Club (all of them were in Golf Digest's top 100 golf courses).

To play these courses, arrangements had to be made through a member of the club, and with our contacts, we achieved a status which merited a short article about us in The Golf Magazine, April 1978, page 21. We named the group the Ecumenical Grand Tour.

Nick Porreca owned the Rivervale Country Club. In the early 60's, I played golf with a guaranteed starting time every Saturday with several of my fraternity brothers, Ted Boutis, Cliff Milton, and Paul Lee.

While playing golf at Rivervale Country Club, I was hired by Nick Porreca to negotiate with the Hackensack Water Company, which planned to build a reservoir adjoining the golf course.

In the original plans, the water company would use condemnation powers to take a portion of the course, encompassing three holes. I argued that the company had to pay for the value of the whole 18-hole course, as a 15-hole course was almost worthless. You can imagine the scene with this little lawyer telling off the big water company lawyers. During a meeting at the Water Company's Headquarters in Weehawken, the president of the company walked into the meeting, His name was Mr. Buck. For all intents and purposes, the Water Company was Mr. Buck, though it was a public company. After introductions, I explained my position. With very little thought, he said to his lawyers and engineers that my position was reasonable. Instead of taking Porreca's land, the company should build a dike around the reservoir. In addition, the company agreed to supply unlimited water from the reservoir.

The construction of the dike proved to be more difficult than originally thought. Raising the water level as high as 30 feet created hydrostatic pressure on the golf course. This required the construction of retaining basins on part of the 14th and 15th holes. This didn't affect the use of the course but added interest to those holes. That is the way the course is today.

Sometime later (maybe in the 70's or 80's), Nick received an offer from the Lehn and Fink Company to buy the course for construction of their headquarters. There were about 120 acres of land, including a small portion owned by the water company under a long-term lease.

You can imagine the extent of those negotiations with big time law firms, accountants, state Public Utilities, and municipal and county governments. After we closed the sale, Lehn had prepared plans and sought the necessary approvals. Then the Kodak Company bought Lehn and Fink and changed their mind to build a headquarters. The golf course was back on the market. Porreca was asked to manage the course until a buyer could be found.

Ultimately, a Japanese company which had bought Pebble Beach Golf Course in California and some others expressed an interest in Rivervale, with its large Japanese following. With the assistance of Porreca, a deal was struck. The course, now owned by a Korean company, remains one of the better public courses in the state.

CHAPTER EIGHT

1959 To 1963

In 1959, I received my first chance to become a Borough Attorney in Cresskill. A fraternity brother and New York Mirror reporter, Rodney Stahl lived in Cresskill and had a friend who was a councilman. I didn't get the appointment then, but two years later, I was appointed. Being a Borough Attorney opened up a whole new phase of law for me.

The importance of this appointment to me was so evident that when, on the night of one of the first meetings, Donna decided to run away from home on a snowy cold night in January, I told Grace I could not be bothered with her. Grace insisted and I eventually found her. This incident shows how distorted our priorities can be.

The experience and exposure I received as Borough Attorney resulted in my being asked to become an Assistant County Counsel for the Board of Freeholders. This led to further exposure and Maywood offered me the Borough Attorney's job in 1963.

In November 1963, I attended the League of Municipalities Convention in Atlantic City, which generally ran from a Tuesday to a Friday of the second week of November. I planned to attend the New Jersey Bar Association convention the same week, from Thursday to Sunday. On Friday that week, while I was heading up the Boardwalk to the Bar meeting, I passed a boardwalk hawker on a pedestal outside a shop soliciting customers. He was abruptly interrupted by a news flash that President Kennedy had been shot in Texas. The initial story didn't say whether he was dead or not. This convinced me to change my mind about the Bar convention, and I headed home.

During the fifties, I was doing real estate closings with the Toomey-Fountain organization in Bergen County, and one of the active builders was Dick Higgins, and Bill and Marion Higgins were active real estate brokers.

In 1960 or 1961, I became an unpaid aide to Marion Higgins, the Speaker of the New Jersey Assembly. Under the laws of New Jersey, she would serve as Acting Governor if the Governor and Senate President were out of state at the same time. When this occurred, she had the use of the Governor's car, with its State Trooper driver.

During the same period, the Legislature embarked on an investigation of a large Green Acre Bond issue expenditure. Marion's husband Bill, a former FBI agent, and I were asked to head the team. We found some irregularities in the appraisal practice but Governor Richard Hughes exercised executive privilege to withhold some documents the committee wanted.

A former Deputy Attorney General had copies of the records I was seeking and gave me access to whatever I needed. Unfortunately the inability of the legislative committee to agree on a report resulted in no action being taken against the wrongdoers.

CHAPTER NINE

1965 To 1969 – Assembly, GOP Convention, Political Activity

Throughout these years, I was involved in Republican politics and formation of UNICO chapters, a national service organization of Italian-Americans. In August 1966, I was installed as President of UNICO National in Santa Monica, California. Then the GOP leaders offered me the opportunity to be a state Assembly candidate. I was elected in 1967 to serve a two-year term for 1968-1969.

My district was the 38th, consisting of Hackensack, Maywood, Rochelle Park, Oradell, Paramus, Lodi, and Bogota, East Paterson (now Elmwood Park) and Garfield.

It might be interesting to reveal how a little Italian kid from Democratic Hudson County became a Republican.

In 1943, my sister, Helen and I served on the Hudson County Republican Committee. The appointments were not because of any particular political passion, but, because Judge Cozzi, for whom Helen worked, was one of the rare Republicans in Hudson County at that time. The district probably had about 10 Republicans with 6 in my family. Most of the job centered on elections, which were Tuesdays, which prevented my sister from any extensive involvement because she played the organ at a St. Anthony Novena in St Rocco's church every Tuesday. After I returned from my military service in 1946, I was again appointed to the Committee.

The Bergen County delegation consisted of 10 assembly members and five senators. One of the senate candidates was "Dick" Dickenson, a major stockholder of the large drug company, Becton-Dickenson. His personal contribution to the campaign was so generous that we could have billboards to the same extent as others had bumper stickers.

The campaign required appearances at meetings of civic and political bodies, as well as standing at shopping centers to give out campaign material. My first team was Grace and the girls. The girls anxiously asked for votes for their father, as they pushed a piece of literature in the hands of prospective voters. On election night, Lisa, then 10 years old, went with me to the headquarters in Maywood and Paramus, then to the Hackensack YMHA stage and a cheering crowd. In many instances she was lost in the crowd and disturbed with the heavy overcast of smoke.

In January 1968, the whole family went to Trenton for the swearing-in ceremony on the floor of the Assembly.

The same year, Frank Buono was elected to the nine-member board of freeholders. We had a major victory in the state and county elections giving the GOP a substantial majority in the State legislature and a six to three GOP Board of Freeholders. The term of Governor Richard Hughes, a Democrat, would run through 1968.

My experience in Trenton is renewed many times as I watch the activities in Congress, with the two houses of legislation, and their committee functions. I personally am aware of the power of the chairman of committees, the Speaker of the House and the political organization, as to which bill would be considered or buried in some innocuous committee.

After you are able to reach a position for a vote on the floor, you had to give consideration to the view of the Senator from your district. Always in the background was the position of the executive branch on the subject matter, with the possibility of a veto.

In 1968, the Meadowland Commission was created to govern the extensive wetlands in Bergen and Hudson Counties. This legislation experienced the procedure set forth above. The Bergen County Assembly delegation insisted on protection of the interest of the towns directly on the land to be included in the Commission.

We met with the Bergen Senate members on a Saturday in Rutherford, just before the Monday when the bill was to be voted on. The 10 votes of Bergen were absolutely necessary for the 57 votes required for this bill. On the Monday, we voted the bill; it was passed in the Senate where Senator Dickenson was the prime sponsor. The Governor conditionally vetoed it, and returned it to the Assembly. At this point only 41 votes were required to approve the legislation, and thus Bergen County could be bypassed.

Probably the most important act by the Commission was the approval of the New York Giants stadium, the Meadowlands Race track and the Byrne Arena, now known as the Continental Arena.

Current proposals presently before the legislature for the Meadowlands included: construction of a sports complex in Newark and a completely changed use for the sports complex.

785 acres of the meadowlands had been proposed for a major industrial, shopping, office, hotel and housing development. Another portion is being considered for three golf courses and multiple use development. Included in this proposal was the dismantling of the garbage transfer station and the complicated closure of the land fill projects (the primary use of the land for the past 50 years or more).

Another statute passed in the same legislative session was one providing for Ramapo College in Bergen County and Stockton College in Atlantic county. The original proposal had been for one school in Northern New Jersey and one in Southern New Jersey. The ultimate locations demonstrated the power of the Bergen and the Atlantic Delegations, the latter under the leadership of the long term Senator "Hap" Farley.

In this story of the state activities, it is important to note the prominence of Nelson Gross as a Republican leader. Gross's influence was fully shown at the National GOP convention in Florida in 1968. The state delegation switched its support from Nelson Rockefeller, millionaire Governor of N.Y., supported by US Senator Clifford Case (N.J.), to Richard Nixon, Gross's candidate.

At the convention Grace's brother Joe hoped that his friend, then Massachusetts' Governor John Volpe, might win the Vice president spot. We were disappointed when it went to Governor Spiro Agnew of Maryland, especially in light of Agnew's later disgrace.

The campaign gave me the opportunity to meet Governor Volpe, Senator Bob Dole (later presidential candidate) and others.

There were many functions at hotels and other public places. At one of these, I posed for a picture with Nixon and his wife, Pat. We were invited to attend the Inauguration, and one of the seven separate balls. One of the County newspapers ran a picture of Grace in her gown. To say the least, it was an exciting event.

Nelson Gross was later appointed by Nixon to serve as an Under Secretary of State for Drug enforcement.

Back in Bergen County, Tony Statile served as the active leader of the party while Nelson was in Washington. With the White House won, the party concentrated on gaining the State House. Under the leadership of Nelson Gross, State GOP Chairman, and Tony Statile, the Bergen County GOP decided to support Bill Cahill, a Congressman from Camden County for Governor.

This selection set up a political dispute within the county as several prominent Republican office holders, including Joe Job, then County Sheriff and Frank Buono, then a Freeholder, supported "Charlie" Sandman, a Congressman from Cape May County.

Governor Cahill, Secy. Transportation John Volpe, MJF

Prior to the Bergen County Republicans' endorsement of Cahill, Frank had received a phone call from Charlie Kraus, a long time

Republican activist and office holder, with a message that Nelson Gross wanted a commitment from Sandman to support Gross's bid for U.S. Senator in the 1970 election. For this commitment, Nelson would support Sandman for Governor. Buono immediately phoned Sandman in Washington to relay the message. Sandman brushed off the suggestion saying "Ha Ha, him and 100 other guys." This comment was relayed back to Nelson through Buono and Kraus. As a result, Gross threw the Bergen County Republican organization's support to Cahill.

Cahill beat Sandman in the June 1969 primary and then defeated former Governor Meyner in the November General election.

Within the inner circle of the Republicans, it was known that Gross wanted to run for U.S. Senate and would be looking for the support of the person in the Governor's chair.

Two weeks after the General Election, Nelson Gross phoned Buono to set up a face-to-face meeting with Sandman. Buono called Sandman in Washington, who said, "I'll fly up tomorrow . . . meet me at Teterboro Airport at noon."

Buono and Gross picked up Sandman at Teterboro and were joined in a restaurant called Club 80 for lunch with Pat Di Zenzo, the political leader in Hackensack, a high school teacher, owner of the restaurant, and other real estate. Gross made his case to Sandman, arguing why he should be the Republican nominee for U.S. Senate in 1970, and asking Sandman for his support. After a short discussion, Sandman pledged his support to Gross.

Gross, Sandman and Buono went to Gross' Office to call the news wire services to announce that Nelson would be the candidate. Gross lost the general election against Democrat Harrison "Pete" Williams, who served in the U.S. Senate for many years.

CHAPTER TEN

1969 To 1972—Politics

My political involvement provided an opportunity to seek other borough attorney and local board appointments. I served as attorney for East Paterson (now Elmwood Park) and Old Tappan; my partner, Frank Glock, represented the Paramus Planning Board.

Dick Mola became the Mayor of East Paterson in 1971 and remained the Mayor until 2005. In 1983, he was elected to the Board of Freeholders and remained in office until December 2000, when he was defeated. He regained his seat after a very difficult election in 2001, in which the Democrats won the Governor's office, control of the Assembly and attained an even split in the Senate.

During this period I became a member of the Republican Party Policy committee that consisted of about 26 or 27 of the leaders of the party in Bergen County.

This group selected candidates for offices from the County level to the state legislative members. It also decided who the County party would support for governor, Congress and President.

During my term in the Assembly, a redistricting took place, putting me and another Republican incumbent into the same district. Concerned about a primary battle, the party asked me to forego another run for the Assembly and take the County Counsel position. It was understood that I could run for the State Senate the next time around. When that time came, I realized how much I preferred the Counsel position and I declined.

During these years, there were federal, state, county and local elections in which I was involved. In 1972, President Nixon was re-nominated for President and his campaign was coordinated with the other elections.

During this campaign, I had the occasion to meet with Bob Dole, then GOP National Chairman, Senator Domenici from Arizona, Governor George Romney and others. John Ingannamorte, then County GOP chairman, owned a twin engine Cessna, which he used to fly various campaigners for President Nixon.

As I said previously, I became County Counsel in June 1969, succeeding Pierre "Pete" Garvin who had been appointed a County judge by Gov. Hughes. During his campaign for Governor, Bill Cahill visited the courthouse and in the process met Pete Garvin.

MJF and Senator Bob Dole

MJF, Gov. George Romney

Senator Baker, MJF

Statile, MJF, Atty Gen Michell

When Cahill was elected, some members of the transition team (including my friend Charlie Kraus) remembered Pete and recommended him for Governor's Counsel. Ironically, the list for that job included my name. (I had said I wasn't interested: it was a hard job, as I knew from the activities of the outgoing Counsel, Van Ness).

How smart was I? Pete took the job and ultimately became Chief Justice of the N.J. Supreme Court. In the interim, while Governor's Counsel, he guided me when I made an application for a bank charter,

Earlier in this story, I mentioned Dick Nelson, County Administrator. I believe he went into County government in the late 1950's or early 1960's. As a reporter, he had met Walter Jones, the powerful state Senator from Bergen County.

Walter's office was across the street from the Court House and the Freeholders office. He had hired another reporter by the name of Bill Kohms. Dick Nelson and Bill became close friends and advisors not only to Jones but also to the Bergen County Republican organization.

Dick, Bill and Charlie Kraus became friends. Charlie Kraus became Supervisor of Roads for Bergen County, and the Clerk to the State Assembly or Senate. Dick became the Clerk to the Board of Freeholders and later County Administrator, running the day to day operation of County government.

In that capacity, he prepared budgets presented to the nine-member Board of Freeholders and effectively established the County tax rate for all of the municipalities in the County. His personality and temperament were the calmest I had ever known and I admired his ability to get things done efficiently. His integrity and knowledge permitted the Freeholders, the County Counsel and all department heads to feel comfortable in carrying out their duties. In addition to his family, Dick loved golf. On the course, he wore sneakers rather than golf shoes. He also bred and trained Labrador Retrievers with his wife of over 50 years, Jane. They have a son and a daughter.

CHAPTER ELEVEN

1969-1976—County Counsel

In 1969, I was sworn in as County Counsel by Judge Peter Ciolino. I served in that capacity until 1976. During that time, I became friendly with Frank Buono who became Chairman of the Freeholders, an extremely important position. We became more than just political friends and to this day we are near neighbors in Florida and socialize there and in New Jersey. At the time of my appointment, the board consisted of nine members elected at large for a 3-year term. The County Counsel was appointed by the board, also for a 3-year term.

In 1973 or 1974, while I was County Counsel, the County needed more office space. 355 Main Street in Hackensack, previously a department store known as Arnold Constable, was vacant.

When Dick Nelson, County Administrator, investigated the ownership, he learned it was being acquired in foreclosure by Paul Schmidt and Jerry Lombardo, owners of the adjoining buildings. The foreclosure was in the Chancery Division of Bergen County before Judge Peter Ciolino, who was being pressed by the foreclosing bank to permit the Sheriff's sale to take place. I appeared before the Judge to assure him the County was interested in buying the property when the necessary bonding procedure for the funds was completed, and without being involved in open bidding at the pending Sheriff sale. Based on that assurance, the Judge delayed the Sheriff's sale. Schmidt and Lombardo completed the purchase from the foreclosing bank, and then conveyed it to the County.

As a result of that matter, I became friendly with Paul who asked me to handle some tax appeals for him.

Some time later, I learned that his long-time secretary, Joyce Galgano, was also the Manager of much of his property. She had started as a superintendent of a garden apartment building on Essex Street, Hackensack.

Paul and Joyce were divorced from their respective spouses. On December 14th, the same day she had been hired by Paul many years before, they were married in 1999. Our friendship has grown, and Grace and I enjoy our golfing with them at Ridgewood Country and in Florida.

As County Counsel, I worked on many major cases. One of lasting significance regarded the Overpeck Creek area in Teaneck, Ridgefield, Palisade Park and Leonia. Some time in the 1950's, those towns had conveyed land bordering the Creek to the County, with the understanding that the County would use it for a park.

In the interim, the land was used partially for a land fill. Another parcel was Overpeck Golf Country Club. There were also several baseball fields and other improvements.

In 1973, the towns brought suit against the County, alleging that the County had failed to develop the land as agreed. The towns wanted the County to either develop the land or return it to them. After extensive litigation, the parties settled. As part of the settlement, the County was required to construct additional parks and make other improvements.

In the spring of 2000, a story develops that a group wants to construct a minor league baseball stadium in the same area. This aroused the public and also the townships involved with the judgment entered in 1973 that was about to expire. An action was filed to extend the judgment and more importantly to force the County to return the lands to them or proceed with construction of the planned park. The towns' original action was dismissed without prejudice on a technical defect; they subsequently filed a new suit, which was settled with the County required to proceed with the park, and concessions given to the towns.

County Executive, Pat Schuber put forth a major project he entitled "Bergen's Central Park", consisting of 785 acres including the minor league baseball stadium proposed by a person who owned a Minor League team playing in Sussex County, and requiring financial participation by the County. As of December 2001, many issues have been raised. The estimated cost is $40 Million and a 6-year plan.

Another matter I handled arose around 1973. The County had embarked on the construction of the Darlington golf course. By law, the County had to accept the lowest responsible bidder. The contract was given to a corporation which had bid $777,777.77 (next closest was $1,200,000). As part of the process, all bidders had to procure a surety bond. Early in the job, it was clear that the winning bidder could not complete the job. I was able to recover $670,000 from the bonding company before I left office in 1976.

Two subsequent contractors were hired and the course was finally completed.

In a recent conversation, I recalled how important Peter Ciolino, County Treasurer (cousin to Judge Peter Ciolino previously mentioned), was to me as County Counsel; he had major responsibility for bonding proposals and reports required by the State. I had complete confidence in his ability and integrity. In recent years Pete's daughter, Roseanne and my daughter Lisa, became close friends, sharing family vacations as well as close frequent contact.

I must also mention Bob Belmonte, the County Purchasing agent and responsible for hundreds of million dollars of the budget. Any action taken by the department was completely documented and could withstand the scrutiny of the severest critics or officials. He was knowledgeable about both the purchasing statutes of the state and the court cases interpreting them.

In 1973 the Democrats won the majority in Maywood, which meant I would lose the position of Borough Attorney. During the Christmas holidays, however, I received a call from politicians in Garfield asking me to consider that city's attorney's job. I wasn't anxious to take on the job as the town was known for political in-fighting. At first, I suggested they ask

Al Schiaffo, a Republican and Magistrate in Lodi and Washington Township. My Garfield contacts convinced me that a recent change in the town's form of government required my particular knowledge and expertise.

The incumbent town attorney was Vinnie Rigolosi, a long time resident of Garfield. Although he fought replacement, in the middle of February 1973, I was appointed. The fight would continue.

In July, Rigolosi filed a law suit alleging my June 1969 appointment as County Counsel was a conflict with the Garfield position, and joined as parties East Paterson since I served as their Borough Attorney (later changed to Elmwood Park), Old Tappan (my associate Steve Spector was covering), and Paramus (where associate Frank Glock was Planning Board attorney was serving), all represented by my office.

Despite favorable case law to our side, I tired of the Garfield in-fighting. I resigned, and the case was dismissed. Rigolosi's brother-in-law, Anthony Schiuto, got the position.

Ironically, when the Democrats gained control of the Freeholders in 1976, there was a dispute between Steve Moses and Vinnie Rigolosi for the County Counsel position. I agreed to cooperate with them and resign in March of the year, although my term ran until June. I was replaced by Vincent Rigolosi, a personal friend of the new Freeholder Chairman Jerry O'Connor.

In 1976 we met Joe and Micki Yackowitz, neighbors of Nick and Doreen Porreca in Ridgewood. Joe worked on Wall Street as a research director for a major stock brokerage firm.

As a courtesy to Nick, he offered me some advice. I had just left the County Counsel and had accumulated about $6,000 in my state pension. I did not intend to go back into government employment again (my story shows how wrong I was).

I withdrew the money and opened an account with his brokerage firm. In the normal course of events, he would not have been involved in individual accounts, except for relatives (I became a brother-in-law).

In the 25 years that I have had this account, it has incurred very few losses. In todays down market, it is worth over $300,000 even with substantial withdrawals over the years. The corporate frauds of 2000 and 2002 caused the first loss.

Long after our meeting, while at dinner Joe mentioned that his first apartment after coming out of the service was in Camp Shanks, New York. In 1947, the barracks were rented by the government to veterans. It was an interesting coincidence, as I was at Camp Shanks in 1944 on my way overseas.

CHAPTER TWELVE

Florida

With Buono and I out of political office, we put our attention to earning a living in our chosen fields: me at law and him in real estate and insurance. At some point, he bought a home in Hillsboro (south of Boca Raton). My friend, Frank Melehan, was building in Jupiter, and friends Paul and Ginny Patti had a place in Boca Raton.

In 1972, I had met the Pattis, during the time I was forming the Bergen Bank of Commerce. Sometime in 1976 or 1977, they invited us for a long weekend at their condominium apartment in Boca Raton. This was an offer hard to refuse. In January 1979, the four of us made the trip. This first visit was delightful; though it was a cold night and Paul did not know how to turn on the heat. We repeated it in one form or another for a couple of years, with some visits as long as two weeks. The apartment was in a building known as the Marbella, on the ocean, with a view of Boca Lake and the famous Boca Hotel. It was a beautiful large apartment, with two bedrooms, two baths and tennis courts across the street.

Paul and I first played tennis at public courts like Van Saun Park. As our interest increased, we joined the Maywood Indoor courts playing doubles with our wives, and then moved to the Quest Courts in Ramsey, and the Washington Township indoor courts. When we went to the Pattis' home in Florida, we used the condo association's courts.

Some time later, the Pattis developed an interest in golf, joining White Beeches Country Club. In 1973, I joined Ridgewood Country Club. Subsequently, we played less tennis and more golf, until we concentrated on golf both in New Jersey and at Royal Palm Country Club in Boca Raton, Florida. We have also had the opportunity to play golf with Ed and Betty Garino, and Paul and Joyce Schmidt at Jonathan Landing in Jupiter, Florida and Frank and Charlotte Joy at Boca Point in Florida.

In Jupiter, Florida, Frank Melehan built "four-plexes"—four units in a square, each with two bedrooms and two baths.

With so many friends in Florida, we began to look for a Florida place of our own for use in the winter. At the same time (in or about 1980), Melehan was building a condo complex in Wyckoff. Because the Maywood house was larger then we needed with our daughters out of the house, Grace and I decided to sell that house, buy a condo in Wyckoff, and find a place in Florida.

Melehan's proposal was to build a complex for persons 55 years or older. The land he wanted to use was owned by Mr. Pulus, who was conducting a small chicken hatchery producing eggs for research. The remaining land was excavated for the gravel, by the Sam Braen Company, which left the 25 acres virtually flat, without any trees or shrubbery.

The plan for Spring Meadow Condominiums called for 112 units, in one—and two-story town houses, a club house and tennis courts. To make the development blend into pretty, suburban Wyckoff, Melehan added fully grown trees, gently rolling berms, attractive landscaping and a curving road plan, with cul-de-sacs.

In Maywood, the master bedroom was on the first floor; in Spring Meadow, it is on the second. When it rains at night, I can be lulled to sleep by the pitter patter of rain drops on the roof, which I hadn't experienced in the 25 years in Maywood. Because I represented Melehan, we could choose any unit we wanted. We even had the surveyor lay out the path of the sun as it related to particular lots and the houses on them. Though the exterior of all the units were uniform, we had some freedom inside, even moving some walls and closets.

As if this major change in our lives were not enough, Grace and I then turned to finding a place in Florida, as well.

Grace and I enjoyed our time in Florida with the Pattis, but felt we were imposing. In August 1980, UNICO was holding its National Convention in Florida. Mixing house hunting with convention activities, we spent a week traveling up and down Palm Beach County, looking on the ocean and inland, in high rises, low rises and on many golf course complexes with a wide range of prices.

This trip sharpened our focus: We wanted to be a short distance from the ocean, where we could drive to a golf course if we wanted. After an extensive search, we saw an eighth-floor apartment in a development called Boca Highlands. The complex was in Highland Beach, bordered on the west by the Intercoastal Waterway, with a marina and a large beach house complex planned across the street on the ocean. The building, Aberdeen Arms, was part of the early phases of development, with more to come.

The apartment had two bedrooms, two baths, a large living/dining room, an eat-in kitchen and a balcony with an expansive view of the Atlantic Ocean, the Waterway and the marina. While we stood on the balcony, looking at the vista, my lovely wife, a.k.a. the Chief Justice, said simply, "Buy it." I suggested we should try to negotiate the price or other conditions. She repeated in a very nice way (as judges sometimes do) "BUY IT".

We signed an offer, which was accepted. The closing was set for November 1980. To help defray expenses, I asked my brother Jerry if he was interested in sharing the apartment. After a weekend at the Patti apartment and a tour of the various locations we had investigated, my brother agreed. We shared the apartment for eight or nine years until an apartment became available across the hall. I bought out Jerry's share, and he bought that unit, which was a mirror image of ours only on the south side of the building.

In 1996 we started looking for a bigger apartment. We wanted more space for our guests, especially our grandchildren. After looking at many locations, up and down in Palm Beach County, we chose another apartment in the same complex: a three-bedroom, three-bath, apartment, with a large southern exposure balcony in Dalton Place. The new apartment, closed in October 1997, nicely furnished, was an easy move, involving only one son-in-law, one granddaughter and a rolling luggage trolley. The picture below is on the terrace of the new apartment.

In 1987, while we were in Aberdeen, the Buonos bought an apartment in the Sea Ranch complex which was across a small inlet from our building.

The Buonos and we have developed a family relationship with a lot of personal contact when we're in Florida. Without any question, however, when Frank introduced me to Web TV, I was hooked: Frank and I became daily correspondents. We do tear ourselves away, to enjoy the annual barbeque that Grace and I host. Along with the Buonos, our first guests included Ignatius and Mella Belgiovine, Frank and Charlotte Joy, and Paul and Ginny Patti.

We started the tradition of the barbeque while living in Aberdeen. It began as a small barbeque for our friends in the area. We picked a nice spot, by the pool which overlooked the Intercoastal. The menu was hamburgers, steak, Italian sausage, salads, desserts (many homemade) with lots of wine and soda. Friends like Neff Rella would help me with the grilling. As the party grew from 10 or 12 to as many as 60, we got professional help and moved to the beach house, which had more grills, tables and chairs. If the weather was bad, we could move the party upstairs to a large room, with a bar, kitchen facilities, and rest rooms. Indoors or out, a party of over 100 people could be accommodated.

The guest list included friends from my political, professional and organization activities, including former Governors William Cahill and Brendan Byrne. The popularity of the party grew to the point it became a topic of conversation in Bergen County when a Florida vacation was talked about. Eventually, guests that I really didn't know began showing up.

While the barbeque was a great way for me to see many friends from Bergen County, I had to agree with the "Chief Justice," that the party had gotten out of hand. Instead of a big bash, we returned to inviting a few couples to a barbeque at the beach house. The wonderful thing about friendship is that this has proved to be as enjoyable as the bigger event.

Grace and I always enjoy Florida, although sometimes, we've had to work around scheduling conflicts. For example, when Bergen County moved to a County Executive form of government in 1984, I was asked by my friend John Ingannamorte, then Bergen County GOP Chairman, to serve as Attorney for the new Legislative Board of Freeholders. Although I happily accepted at first, I had second thoughts. It was November and we had planned to go to Florida the next week. I called John back saying I would agree to accept the following spring.

Unfortunately, my appointment had already been announced to the press. There was an extensive new Administrative Code to be adopted within the next four months. My experience was important to the board members involved in the deliberations. When this news was broken to the "Chief Justice," she was not happy, but as usual she supported my decision.

From 1986 until about 1996, I arranged our Florida trips on a two-week commuting basis, missing only one work session of the board each month. Then, in February 1996, New Jersey was hit with a 25-inch snowfall that closed the airports. Although I was scheduled to return to New Jersey, Bill Van Dyke, Chairman of the Board of Freeholders, discouraged me from attempting it. If it were he, Bill said, he would not try to come back.

If this was good enough for the Chairman, I had no problem agreeing, and arranged for one of my partners to cover the meeting. In the weeks that followed, there were heavy snowfalls almost every week, several closing the airports on the very day I was scheduled to fly to New Jersey. Each time, Dennis Harraka, one of my partners stepped in.

This proved to be a very enjoyable arrangement for me. The Board agreed to accommodate me for the first three months of each year. In December 2000, when the Democrats became the majority party of the Board, the question became moot.

CHAPTER THIRTEEN

Christmas Shopping

In 1962, shortly before Christmas, I decided to take the girls to a large discount department store called E.J. Korvettes (which stood for "Eight Jewish Korean Veterans, I am told"), not far from our house in Maywood. Like now, stores would hold special clearance sales. As we wandered the store, we listened to the special deals announced on the loud speakers. Items might be priced at a penny or a nickel, but only for 10 minutes or so. We'd rush to the announced department to get the item. As our pile of loot grew, we couldn't carry it around. Our solution was to have Lisa, then not quite six years old, guard the packages as we ran around the store. In those days, we didn't worry about leaving Lisa and packages alone.

This insane expedition was made for several years, allowing all of us (including my sophisticated older daughters) to enjoy toys and games they might have considered too juvenile. I also enjoyed the trucks, trains and cars that previously we had "forgotten" to give our daughters.

As long as I am at Christmas, I should mention the many Christmas Eves spent assembling doll carriages, toy kitchens, bicycles and other surprises from Santa. It was a race to complete the process before the girls awoke (which was often at five or six in the morning). In at least one case, I finished the job barely minutes before the patter of little feet sounded on the stairs. More than once, I had to shoo them back upstairs telling them that Santa had not arrived yet.

One year, Grace said she wanted a peck of diamonds and a bushel of gold. Such a request was not going to be a problem for this big shot. I placed a nice red brick, painted gold and a few shining glass baubles in a nicely wrapped box. I don't recall what happened to the gems, but the gold brick was a doorstop in Maywood for years.

Procrastination was my typical mode during the holidays. On the afternoon of Christmas Eve, I would run to Florence Shop to pick up gifts for Grace, about none of which I knew. My job was simply to call Bill Merten, the interior decorator at the store, who would pick out items he knew Grace would like. The presents would be beautifully wrapped, waiting for me. I would be as surprised as Grace on Christmas Day.

This relationship with the Florence Shop continued in one fashion or other as accountant or lawyer for more than 40 years. The record will show, Florence Shop became the mainstay of the wardrobe of the women of my life as well as me. Florence Eberhardt and Bill Merten, the interior decorator of the store, were valued advisors to Grace and to me. The store grew from a narrow little dress shop to a chic multi-floor department store. Through all this time, I had my gift giving covered: whether it was women's apparel or furnishings for the house, Bill and Florence could come up with ideas guaranteed to please Grace and me.

After Florence Eberhardt died and Bill Merten retired to Florida, Florence Shop closed and Grace found it necessary to find other shops for her wardrobe. As luck would have it Nordstrom opened in the Garden State Plaza. We learned they had personal shoppers available to assist customers.

On our first visit to the store, we met Marie Feinbloom. After learning she had been born in Jersey City of Italian parents, and that her father died when she was very young, I was struck by the similarity to my own life. I also told her the story of Bill Merten.

If she could be as good as he was, my life as well as my wife's would be a lot easier. She has proven to be just as effective for us and our daughters. I must add Joseph John and I have become Nordstrom customers. Did we have much choice?

In the early years in Maywood, we would invite neighborhood children of all faiths to help us trim the tree. Even on our tight budget, Grace managed a little gift for each of them. One of the more prosperous years (I think it may have been 1955), I bought a new Ford Station wagon, placed a big red bow on the roof and drove it from the dealer to home.

Our Christmas tradition called for Grace, me and the girls (dressed in matching outfits) to travel to Ozone Park and Grandpa Deliso's house. In the early years of our married lives, we joined 20 or more relatives. The high point of the trip for the children was lining up (Ferraras, Caruanas, Johnsons, Cenigilios, and Delisos) to get a brand new $2 bill from Grandpa. Grace tried to get in line one year but her father said" no good". In addition, the large living room was stacked with gifts.

For me, the best part of the day was the full Italian meal. The Caruanas, who lived in the two family house with my father-in-law and his second wife, (my mother-law had died in 1950) set up an enormous table of plywood and sawhorses in the basement. Everyone enjoyed salads, spaghetti, anti-pasta, meatballs, pork and other specialties – and these were only the appetizers! The main course would call for veal cutlets, vegetables, roast meat or turkey, potatoes and bread. Desserts were Italian cheesecake, pastries, fruit and nuts, followed by espresso and coffee and Grandpa's homemade wine.

The family came from Long Island, New Jersey and Massachusetts. The usual participants included the families of Grace's brothers John and Mary Deliso, Mike and Frances Deliso. Anne and Al Cenigilio, Mary and Gerald Johnston, and of course, Rose and George, who lived at the house. As the children got older, the Christmas event grew smaller. But looking back, it brought wonderful memories.

CHAPTER FOURTEEN

1972 To 1989—Bergen Bank

In the early 1970's, Frank Reiger and John Gabriel approached me with the idea of forming a new bank. I was intrigued by the idea and we agreed to each seek three other business men we thought strong enough to be incorporators. I would be Chairman of the Board of Directors and co-counsel with Rieger.

Our incorporators included John and Michael Ingannamorte, my brother Jerry, Paul Patti and his brother, Joe, John Borreson, Connie Imming, and several others. In the process, I met many businessmen who, to this day, continue to be friends.

Our initial capital was $1,200,000. We started the bank in two trailers and within a year built a new two story building on Midland Avenue Paramus, with the bank on the ground floor and my office on the second floor.

To obtain a charter, it was necessary to satisfy the Commissioner of Banking of the need for a new bank serving the community. A vigorous objection was raised by the Midland Bank. The majority stockholder was the very powerful former state Senator, Walter Jones. At the time of our application, the president of Midland Bank was another former Senator from Camden. They exercised all the possible political influence, including telling our prospective landlords that we would not be able to get a charter and the deal would die.

Despite these dirty tricks, we persevered, with a financially and locally strong list of incorporators. We had to accept the condition that the Midland Bank could open a branch about 300 feet from our location on Midland Avenue and Route 17 in Paramus, and increase our stockholders to approximately 30 members.

The formation of the bank fulfilled a long time desire on my part. When I worked with Toomey-Fountain mortgage business, I realized the importance of being the banker. However I was too busy making a living by closing house sales for $150, of which $50 was for me.

Sitting on the Bank Board gave me the opportunity to use my accounting and legal knowledge, as well as what I had learned during my years with the Toomey Fountain Mortgage Company. I could analyze financial statements to determine the ability of builders to complete projects. Similar review was necessary when retail and manufacturing companies were seeking loans.

The small size of our bank was an advantage, as we could approve loans quickly—in some instances on a conference call or an impromptu meeting. Often, loan officers and board members knew loan applicants personally.

The 12 incorporators provided the initial capital for the bank, $1,200,000. The New Jersey Banking Department insisted on a larger, more diverse shareholder base, so we offered stock to others, expanding to about 30 owners. Our first President was a young man from Florida, Paul Kane, and Chet March, as Vice-President. Chet had a long history in banking and lived in Glen Rock. After one year and the construction of our first building, it became apparent that Paul Kane did not have enough experience to be President of a growing bank.

In our search we were introduced to Ed Halsch who lived in Paramus and was Executive Vice President of a Hudson County bank with which we were familiar. He was hired and remained with us for a few years. Personalities developed and we decided to make a change.

Fred Simken succeeded Ed as President. He had been a popular executive vice-president of the United Bank and was very active locally. The bank's capital was at $22 million when he came on board and through his term increased to about $54 million.

In the summer of 1973 or 1974, Frank Rieger invited the Board of Directors and bank officers to a barbeque at his summer home in Point Pleasant. The food was abundant with steak and lobster as the main course. We all thanked Frank for the party, but he responded that he was thankful we took the trouble to drive to the shore on this beautiful day. He added, there could not be a party without guests. I have remembered and repeated that philosophy many times.

Shortly after the bank opened, we created a branch in the new Paramus Park shopping center. Though not a very profitable branch, it did handle large deposits and exposed the bank to the customers and merchants in the mall.

The board of directors had agreed to serve without compensation. They were permitted and, in some instances, urged to attend national meetings of The American Banking Association, which included banks of all sizes.

In 1977, the Pattis and we decided to go to a conference in Scottsdale, Arizona. After attending interesting meetings on the duties of small bank directors, we rented a car and drove to the Grand Canyon. The view was awesome: snow covering the north side of the canyon with mild weather on the south side.

Having come from the warm weather of Arizona we were not prepared for the cold. The road through the mountains of Arizona was barren and we were advised to be sure we had adequate gas as the service on the road would be limited. At one cross road,

we stopped at a general store gas station. While there, we saw several Jeeps and similar trucks stopped with heavily bearded hunters with an assortment of guns.

Returning to Phoenix, we then flew to Los Angeles. After sightseeing, we took a 4-day bus trip along the Pacific coastline to San Francisco. Along the way, we visited the famous Hearst Castle. It was exquisite, with a large indoor pool, ballrooms, kitchens, numerous bedrooms and other recreational facilities. The gardens were similar to those of European castles.

CHAPTER FIFTEEN

Daughters

This part is not strictly chronological, but addresses our daughters in age order: Virginia, Donna, and Lisa. No favoritism, just the order of how we met them.

Virginia

When Virginia was ready for school in 1955, we had decided to move to Maywood. There she could attend Our Lady Queen of Peace. To ease her into the schedule, we enrolled her in September, before we moved. From September to November, when we moved to Maywood, Grace would drive her to and pick her up after school.

A few years later, the Archdiocese of Newark decided to build several Catholic High Schools. The pastor guided me down the aisle after one mass, inviting me to dinner in the rectory. He asked me to head a special gift committee to solicit contributions for the construction of several new high schools.

Paramus Catholic High School was one of the new schools, and in 1965, Virginia was a member of the first class enrolled. Uncertain about what she wanted to do in college, she enrolled in a junior college, Elizabeth Seton in Yonkers, New York. I became President of the Father's Council. The first issue confronting me was the issue of visits by boys to the girls' dormitory. All of the usual arguments were put forth, "Don't you trust us?", "Anything we could do inside, we could do outside", etc. The Fathers' Council's response was that we parents had selected this school because it was all girls with specific restrictions and that the privacy of all the girls had to be considered as well.

After Elizabeth Seton, Virginia went on to Marymount College in Tarrytown, New York, a beautiful school in a lovely setting overlooking the Hudson River. In 1973, after graduation, she started teaching Art at Assumption School in Emerson, a job she held for about 10 years. About 1994, she was able to get a job in the Ridgefield Public school system as a Special Education Art Teacher. She teaches classes from kindergarten to eighth grade. At this time (2008), she continues to work there and has earned her Master's Degree in Special Education.

Virginia married Michael McNamara on April 24, 1976 at Our Lady Queen of Peace Church in Maywood. The reception took place at Ridgewood Country Club where I have been a member since 1973. They bought a house on Davis Avenue in Hackensack with the assistance of Frank Buono's real-estate company. Michael worked for New York Bell, traveling to Brooklyn. He was able to arrange a transfer to New Jersey Bell which improved his commute.

On May 31, 1981 our first grandchild, Elizabeth Anne, was born, adding another female to my life.

As a result, Virginia and Michael decided a larger home was necessary. My longtime client, Frank Joy, had purchased a ranch style house on Hasbrouck Boulevard, Oradell as an investment. The three bedroom, two bathroom house, situated on a 75 by 150 foot lot, is still their home.

Elizabeth Anne now has her own apartment in Hoboken, New Jersey.

Donna

Donna followed Virginia to Queen of Peace in Maywood and graduated with top honors. She decided to go to Immaculate Heart Academy in Washington Township, also an all girls' Archdiocesan school. She maintained high grades through the four years. Upon graduation, she expressed an interest in theater.

In 1971, Donna entered Roger Williams College in Bristol Rhode Island as a Theater Major. She graduated in 1975 and received an invitation to apply for a Rhodes scholarship from the New England District, the first year it was opened to women. Unfortunately, two Harvard girls were chosen, to display to the world, the Scholarship was not discriminating.

Donna's activities in the theater continued with summer stock in New England, theater on Long Island, and her own theater program in New York and Hoboken (where she had moved). She induced me and a few friends to finance an off-off-Broadway show on 18th Street in New York.

When she tired of endless rounds of auditions, she decided to go into another type of theater: law school. She was successful on her first try and was accepted in June 1979 to New York Law School.

At the end of first year, she was chosen for law review. In December of her third year, she received job offers from various large corporations such as Exxon, Con Edison and New Jersey Public Utilities along with several large law firms. Before graduation, she accepted an offer at LeBouef Lamb Leiby and MacRae, a large firm with its main office in New York.

She graduated in May and take the bar exam in July. The firm offered a $2000 clothing allowance, which she thought could be better used for a Hawaiian vacation with one of her classmates.

In August 1982, she started at LeBouef, which had a reputation in public utilities, litigation and insurance. She developed an expertise in insurance, a field in which she practices to this day. Her practice continued at two insurance companies, then Shearman & Sterling, a global law firm.

At one point, Donna, certain that she would not marry or have children, gave herself, (we will have to check the books), a thirtieth birthday bash to compensate. Shortly after her 31st birthday, however, Raymond S. Carroll entered her life. By 1984, Raymond had convinced her to marry him. The ceremony took place at Windows on the World in the World Trade Center in New York City. Our dear old friend Father Ed Kearney officiated. The reception was held a few steps away on the other side of the Restaurant. It was clear that Donna was not going to follow the Ridgewood Country Club circuit, and even considered the Queen Mary cruise ship as the location of the wedding, etc. Donna and Raymond went off on their honeymoon for a couple of weeks in Europe.

They rented a beautiful apartment on the 25th floor of Marine View Towers in Hoboken overlooking the Hudson River and the skyline of New York. It proved to be an outstanding location to see the Macy's July 4th fireworks display, the Tall Ship parade and many beautiful cruise ships.

A few years later, they moved north to Troy Towers, a cooperative in Union City again overlooking the Hudson River and New York. It was a large 2-bedroom, 2-bath unit, with a large enclosed balcony easily used as another room. In 1992, they later purchased an adjoining 1-bedroom apartment for use as an office for Raymond and a home for a nanny. They needed the nanny for their new addition, Brigitte Grace Ferrara Carroll.

As Brigitte got older, the issue of school districts became important. Ray and Donna wanted Brigitte to attend a good public school, and they undertook an extensive (and I mean extensive) three-year search in Morris, Passaic, Union and Bergen Counties.

Fortunately for us, they found a large 5-bedroom, 3-bath house on a one acre wooded lot just one mile from our home in Wyckoff. Though it had no view of the New York skyline, it was big enough to accommodate all the Ferraras and Carrolls. This, along with the outstanding ability of Donna and Raymond to host a party, made the new place much more enjoyable.

As nice as all of this is, it doesn't compare with the enjoyment of our third grandchild being close enough for a bicycle ride with her father to our house, to enjoy frequent visits for Gram's Tortellini, or fresh mozzarella or to help her grandparents with the computer.

Lisa

Lisa followed her sisters in Queen of Peace, and to some extent had to confront the story of her sisters' activities while in school. She chose Immaculate Heart Academy, as had Donna.

Lisa graduated from IHA, and after looking into various colleges, she decided on New York Institute of Technology in Hempstead, New York. Her major was Communication Arts with emphasis on television news. Though she didn't pursue that career, her training reflects itself in her assistance in my video operations. On graduation, to my surprise, she expressed an interest in law school. She tried it but decided there was a much better road to travel.

Lisa met a fine young man, Joseph Palmeri, while she was at IHA and he was at Bergen Catholic. She had played a role in a Bergen Catholic production of the play *Fiddler on the Roof* and he played the piano. This latter attribute proved to be an enjoyable trait to me as I had a piano in my house all my life, (my sister as you may recall, played the organ in church) and Joseph could play a few tunes for me while waiting for Lisa to get dressed to go out. This compared to being required to drink a glass of wine with Grace's father while waiting for her.

I later learned of Joseph's many other fine attributes, from his detailed knowledge of electronic equipment, such as my video editing and laptop computer and (more low tech, but just as impressive) his ability to install storage cabinets (with grandson Joseph Michael's help) in our Wyckoff garage. To top it all off, he is an outstanding travel agent.

There is a story about Lisa and Joseph's engagement which has become part of family lore: To celebrate their engagement, Joseph's parents invited us for dinner. When it came time for dessert, I was handed a printed menu. As I recall, the list included Peach Melba, parfaits, sundaes, pie and Italian pastries. I assumed they were kidding, and joked (as I often do) that I would have one of each starting with the Peach Melba, then a strawberry sundae, apple pie ala mode, and Italian pastry. To my complete surprise, they had made all of them and started to bring them out. I had to quickly call for help. Ann and Joe Palmeri had heard the story of how I answer waitresses listing desserts and decided to call my bluff.

Joseph and Lisa were married in St. John's Church in Hillsdale in a unique and memorable ceremony. The wedding of our youngest daughter would have been memorable in any event, but leave it to Joseph and Lisa to add something truly remarkable. Of course, Lisa was a radiant and lovely bride, the focus of all attention. Joseph, however, managed to play a more important role than the passively, appreciative groom. In the middle of the ceremony, he walked to the organ and played a song that he had written for Lisa, as she lovingly looked on.

The newlyweds bought a condominium in Rockland County, New York. Lisa traveled to Seton Hall Law School in Newark, New Jersey, and Joseph to Merrill Lynch in New York City.

Lisa attempted to continue law school, but again God's hand made her wishes known. In January 1983, the first new male came into the family as our second grandchild Joseph Michael Ferrara Palmeri was born.

They continued to live in Rockland County for a couple of years and took an active role in the condo association. First Lisa and then Joseph served as President. This was fun for a while, but in a few years, they decided to come back to New Jersey. Joseph's commute to New York City from Bergen County is shorter than from Rockland County.

After much looking, they found a builder who owned a lot in Glen Rock New Jersey. The lot had previously been a right-of-way for Public Service Trolley cars as well as electrical, gas and sewer easements. The overall size of the lot was about 155 feet wide and 350 plus feet deep but the easements made the buildable part of the lot irregular in shape. Though the lot size could have supported a large house, the shape meant the width of the house could not be more than 39 feet.

After some angst, the builder managed a wonderful center hall colonial, well located on the plot. The lot, perfectly landscaped, looks beautiful. Most importantly, the house has been a happy home for Lisa, Joseph and Joseph Michael for many years.

Now, Joseph Michael has his own home in Pennsylvania and it is already showing the gentle touch and good taste of his parents.

CHAPTER SIXTEEN

1986 To 2000—Freeholder Attorney

As I mentioned earlier, in the chapters on Florida and my political life, in November 1986 my political life changed with a call from John Ingannamorte, Bergen County GOP Chairman. I became the attorney for the County Board of Freeholders and helped a new form of County government take shape. This required many changes in governance beginning with a major Administrative Code. During the 14 years I served as Freeholder Counsel, I took part in some major projects.

One task which fell to me was the new administration building. I was involved in extending the lease of the Sanzari building on the corner of Main and Essex Streets in Hackensack being occupied by the County and with the complex agreement with the state Economic Development Administration (EDA). This deal required a "sale" of the building to the EDA, with a lease back to the County for 27 years. At the end of the lease, the Country will get the building back for $1.

This arrangement permitted the County to construct a new building without issuing bonds for the construction. Further, the EDA charged a below market rent of about $18.25 per square foot, compared to Sanzari's request of $23.00 per square foot. In addition, the Sanzari building was an old structure building of 160,000 square feet; the new building would be 260,000 square feet. For the first time in all my years of involvement in many County and private projects, my name was included on the plaque in the lobby of the building.

I was also involved with the transfer of the Bergen Pines Hospital to a private operator, once more, by way of a complicated lease to a County agency known as The Bergen County Investment Authority (BCIA) with a sub-lease to the Solomon Organization, a Colorado nursing home operator.

The unique aspect of our deal was that the hospital actually had three hospitals: a 600 bed geriatric care unit, a 300 bed psychological unit and 175 regular bed hospital unit. Valley Hospital in Ridgewood took over the hospital, another operator, Horizon, the psychological units and Solomon the nursing home units. It now operates as the Bergen Regional Medical Center.

To attempt to set out the extensive negotiations, publicity, litigation, state approvals which took place would require several added chapters to this story, so I'll leave it as it is.

A new jail was also needed. During the 1980's and 1990's, mandatory sentencing was imposed federally. At the same time, the state Legislature was increasing the mandatory jail sentencing crimes including incarceration of fathers and husbands defaulting on court ordered support payments. The County was told to plan a jail with capacity for 1000 to 1600 prisoners.

An excerpt from a New York Times article describes the situation: *"In Bergen, the original jail, a 1910 building, was condemned by the state but had to be kept open until the early 1990's to take prisoners. An annex was built in 1963 to ease overcrowding, but by the late 1980's was sleeping a hundred inmates on the gym floor.* By September 1996, when ground was broken for the new jail, the annex was above capacity.

In 1981, 150 inmates rampaged through the annex, set fire to mattresses and held two guards hostage. They were eventually released unharmed. A report released by the prosecutor's office blamed faulty inmate evaluations, substandard conditions and lack of common sense steps, like removing prisoners' shoelaces. In 1988, the state Office of Inmate Advocacy filed a class action suit complaining the living conditions were unconstitutional. There were many violent outbreaks in 1987. Four inmates committed suicide between April 1991 and February 1992. A survey showed the jail's suicide rate was four times the national average.

In preparing for the jail, the County sought out several experts in the field of jail capacity, construction and management. The original estimate was about $45 million. It then was determined that the Sheriff's Bureau of Criminal Identification had to be enlarged to relieve the delay caused by processing the information through the State Police.

The organization we finally hired had extensive experience. There were many obstacles to overcome, however. Approval of the state Department of Correction (DOC) and the Department of Environment (DOE) were required. As construction proceeded, new requirements were imposed.

Before construction had gone far, the City of Hackensack instituted suit to stop it, alleging zoning restrictions. The City suggested that the jail should be built in the Meadowlands, notwithstanding the fact that the land proposed was protected wet lands, the site was far from the court house and police facilities and there were no social services in that area. In addition, the Public Advocate presented complaints from the prisoners, ranging from frivolous to severe. It took tremendous pressure from the court to effect a settlement permitting construction of the jail.

The cost had escalated to over $60 million. The new jail may quickly become inadequate, as more immigrant detainees, federal and state prisoners are housed there.

During this same period of time, the DOC was under pressure in other parts of the state and constructed a new jail in Essex County near the airport and another near Camden.

I stepped down when the Democrats took control of the Freeholders in 2000.

In November 2001, the election of Dick Mola and Lou Tedesco gave the Republicans control of the Freeholder Board. They asked if I would like my old job back. As tempting as it was, I thanked the members and decided to continue my retirement.

That year, I was invited to the annual County Christmas party by a young, dedicated and active Republican, Margaret Cenci Fronteri. This was my first opportunity to visit the new administration building. In walking into the lobby of the building, I saw the plaque with the names of those involved in the building, which included mine as Counsel to the Freeholders.

To my surprise, when I walked into the party room (the new caucus meeting room), I was greeted with cheers by some of the long time staff. Even the Democrats, including Freeholder Valerie Huttle and their chief-of-staff, joined in.

Toni Fontana, who was the long time Chief Clerk of the board, gave me a tour of the freeholders' quarters including the office I had laid out for myself but never got to use. During this visit, Anthony Casino asked if I would administer the oath of office to him as Chairman of the new Board of Freeholders. I was pleased to do so.

CHAPTER SEVENTEEN

1989—40th Wedding Anniversary

Grace and I celebrated our 40th wedding anniversary in 1989. While the July 23rd anniversary itself was quiet, we commemorated the event with a three week tour of Europe. Our daughters assigned the task of chaperoning us to Donna and Raymond.

We flew First Class to London, thanks to Donna's frequent flier miles. We visited the museums, Buckingham Palace, London Tower, Harrods, Fortnum and Mason, Parliament and Big Ben and took an overall taxi tour of the city, including Piccadilly Square and 10 Downing Street. At the British Museum, we enjoyed the Rosetta Stone and the marvelous Egyptian exhibits.

We took the hydrofoil from Southampton to Calais, France. It was exciting to see the White Cliffs of Dover as we left and on arrival, the same shores of France where the Allies landed in June 1944. We took the bullet train to Paris, through the northern wine country and other farming areas. On the train there was a group of Scots, revved up for a soccer match, which added a degree of entertainment.

In Paris, we toured the Eiffel Tower, Notre Dame, the Louvre, the Arc de Triumph, the Opera house, and made a special trip to the Palace of Versailles. The Palace is exquisite with the famous Hall of Mirrors, Hall of Statues with Venus de Milo and the gardens. I was able to see where I was stationed during my time with the Eisenhower Headquarters. The barracks were actually in the living quarters in the stable area.

We took a nice train ride through France to Bern, Switzerland and stayed at the magnificent Bellevue Plaza Hotel .It was adjacent to the Swiss Parliament Building, on a cliff with an outstanding view. The city tour was enlightening. We saw the walls of the city and how the town was called Bern (sometimes spelled "Berne"). Bern is derived from "beren" which means bears in German. According to legend, the founder of the city killed a bear at the place where the city was founded and honored the entire species with the name of the city. True or not, there are bears on the city flag, on the clock tower, (the Zytglogge) and in the bear pits on the edge of town, where the big, furry creatures loll around, eating peanuts and ice cream thrown by admiring tourists.

The highlight of our time in Switzerland was Zermatt. This mountain town seems straight from the *Heidi* stories. No cars are allowed in the city, and horse drawn carriages are available for the lazy and the romantic. Our hotel, the Hotel Julian, had flower boxes in the windows, balconies overlooking the town and the Matterhorn, luxurious down comforters and scrupulously clean accommodations. Meals were served in many small rooms each with a roaring fireplace.

We took a "rack" train into the Alps. The name comes from the gear-driven traction system. We traveled to the base of the Matterhorn, which took an hour. The view from the train was beyond belief – and the best we had experienced, until we reached the hotel at the end of the track.

Though it was not yet winter, crystal clear snow sparkled along the way. Small towns and hotels dotted the landscape. Hikers and bicyclists enjoyed the lower part of the trip, and skiers the higher part.

In the best Swiss tradition, at the end of the tracks, there was a comfortable restaurant, rest rooms, photos and artwork of the slopes of the Matterhorn. Ray and Donna declared this area one of the best places in Europe to kiss. Grace and I agreed.

After Zermatt, we took a train through the Alps and the Italian Lake country, through Emiligia Romano to Venice.

I must confess my memory of specific sites was fuzzy, so I reviewed some of the 14 hours of video I taped on that trip.

Venice is one of the most amazing and photographed places on earth. Even so, there is nothing to compare with St. Mark's Square with its famous pigeons and the clock tower with the man hitting the bell at the 9 o'clock hour. There were the Palace of the Doges, boat ride on the great canal with views of homes and churches, the market place, the gondolas and a visit to the islands of Murano to see glass making and Burano for lace products and many other things too numerous to name.

Our next stop was Florence, the Ponte Vecchio, lined with jewelry, clothing and antique stores, the Pitti Palace with its ornate rooms, the Academia with the statue of David.

We went on to Rome and visited the Vatican, the Sistine Chapel with the beautiful ceiling painted by Michelangelo, The Forum, the Spanish Steps, Trevi Fountain, the ruins of ancient Rome and many others.

We also had a visit with Luiagina Deliso. Grace's father married Luiagina after Grace's mother died. We had arranged a meeting at the home of one of Luiagina's nieces who lived in Rome. She insisted on giving us a large bottle of a cordial which we had to surrender when leaving Milan. We walked through Rome with the two ladies.

After Rome, we went to Milan and visited the many sites including the famous Cathedral, the Opera House and the original covered shopping mall called the Galleria.

A day before we were to leave Europe, we went back to Switzerland to recover our VAT (value added tax) which I believe was in the area of $300 or $400. This required a one-day train trip to Lugano. The relatively simple VAT task (which required showing the receipts to a border guard) was a little more complicated with some additional shopping.

While the others were shopping, I decided to go in front of the camera like a newscaster to recite the history leading up to our trip, including some examples of the hotels we used, places we visited, and the traveling experience of our "Italian mustache guide" (our Irish son-in-law Raymond) who did a tremendous job!

CHAPTER EIGHTEEN

1999—50ᵗʰ Wedding Anniversary

The conversations with our daughters preceding this event were even more extensive than before the 40ᵗʰ Anniversary. We talked about many ways to commemorate this event ranging from a large party at Ridgewood Country Club, a party at the Spring Meadow club house, a smaller dinner at Ridgewood Country Club with the family and a few friends, to a trip to the Catskills, Poconos, Hershey, a villa in Italy, a cruise to Bermuda or the Caribbean and probably a few others I can not remember.

The factors we considered were the nature of our family, the ages of the grandchildren, the statement by the "Chief Justice" that she preferred to spend the time with our whole family and the fact that with a party of friends we would end up with many gifts we didn't need and a cost of substantial proportions.

Finally, we decided on a two-week trip to Walt Disney World in Florida. Grace and I would provide the basic costs of transportation by air, living accommodations, and general food requirements. This proved to be an outstanding decision. Lisa and Joseph were Disney experts. They prepared a booklet with daily itinerary giving consideration to the different desires of the members of the family.

During the trip, we had special treatment by Continental Airlines and Walt Disney World. We had arranged for two condos with the McNamara and the Carroll/Ferrara in one unit, and the Palmeris and Grace and I in another. Each unit had two bedrooms, two baths, a kitchen, living room with TV, a laundry room and a porch overlooking a golf course and daily maid service.

We rented two vans for transportation to and from the particular parks. Joseph arranged walkie-talkies to keep in contact while in the parks. Before leaving on the trip, the girls purchased red polo shirts and hats embroidered with "Ferrara 50ᵗʰ Anniversary". Ann Carroll (Raymond's sister) gave us similar blue shirts, so we could alternate. We were easy to track in the crowded parks.

The basic understanding of the trip was that individuals could do what they wanted, except for specific meeting times and places (usually meals). With customary efficiency, Lisa and Joseph made arrangements for these family meals. At almost all meals, there were cakes, candles and other festivities for our anniversary.

One day, we were shown to an area roped off for viewing the daily parade at a point where it stopped. The "cast members" (Disney talk for the parade performers) broke off and danced with us.

I will not further elaborate this memorable trip; it is memorialized in 14 hours of tape.

Before going to Disney on July first, we had thought of renewing our vows at regular Sunday Mass. The pastor said the Masses were all taken on the day requested, but we could arrange for a special afternoon 50th Anniversary Mass after we returned from Florida.

We had four days to arrange it. Of course, the girls suggested that if we were having a special Mass, we'd have to invite some friends and then provide a bite to eat. The church organist was going off to Europe. I was fortunate to get him at Mass the night before to give him the music we wanted.

We talked about the invitations and the first thing we knew, the little party, we almost didn't have, reached 70 or 80 invitations. Lisa and Joseph did the invitations, so we didn't know the final count. The Spring Meadow club house could fit 40 or 45, so we decided to put a tent over the club house deck.

Before I left for Florida, I contacted a company, agreed on the size of the tent and the date, our anniversary, the 23rd of July. When I returned from Disney two weeks later, I called to confirm the tent arrangements and was told it wasn't finalized without a deposit. I sent the check, arranged for large fans on the deck, and finalized catering arrangements. The day before the party, Lisa ordered table flowers and balloons.

When I called Father Kearney to confirm his officiating at the Mass and attendance at the party, he remarked (as he often had) that Grace deserved a medal for putting up with me for 50 years. This planted a seed. On the Saturday of the Mass, I wanted to get a medal for Grace.

I had in mind some little toy from a party store, but came up empty. Joseph's sister Lucia suggested a trophy store in Allendale. At 11:00 AM, I called. They closed at 1:00 PM. I dashed there, and picked up an enormous Olympic-style medal. Grace was completely surprised when I hung the heavy disc over her neck at the end of the ceremony.

Our friend Dora Sharpe had arranged for a Papal Blessing certificate to be presented by our pastor, Monsignor O'Leary.

We had a wonderful ceremony, with our older grandchildren taking part in the Mass; Joseph reading and distributing Communion, while Elizabeth and Brigitte brought up the Gifts. Our friends and family shared in our celebration, laughing along with the stories Father Kearny told. We left the church and drove the short distance to Spring Meadows in our car, festooned with ribbons and a "Just Married" sign.

The weather on that day was in the nineties, which strained the Spring Meadow clubhouse air-conditioning and fans. It had been decorated by the girls and our friend Billy Gambino supplied potted and hanging plants. The caterer had done an excellent job.

The best gift, arranged by our daughters, was a memory book, a binder full of letters and stories from our guests.

**Chris Caruana, Virginia, Alice Dolci,
Joseph, Lisa, Nardy Dolci**

CHAPTER NINETEEN

Deliso Family

Because my life is so entwined with Grace's, this book should include some description of her family. Her parents, Clement Deliso and Virginia Migliore, had nine children who lived to adulthood: Joseph, John, Mike, Charlie, Benny, Ann, Grace, Mary, and Rose.

Her family was in the construction business, although at some point, they had a farm in Ozone Park where they lived. The oldest boys entered into the family business and developed an expertise in sewer construction. They honed their skills on Long Island, a place that had a high water table to overcome,

Sometime in the late 1930's, the company was successful in a bid to install a sewer project in Springfield, Massachusetts. The men, Joe and John, rented a house in Springfield during the week and came home on weekends. Early in the 1940's, the boys moved to Springfield. A foundry was acquired by Joe, known as Hampden Brass, with Ben and Charlie working to implement the war production requirements of World War II.

Brass was an important commodity in the war effort. Because of this, the workers received deferments of military service. The brothers, Joe and John, also acquired a tool factory in Worcester known as "Stevens Walden". Brother Mike worked at this facility. On his way to becoming the wealthiest member of the family, Joe acquired several other businesses – a television station, ski resort, frozen food company and others – often with the participation of his brothers.

Joe and his wife Jennie had five children: Clement, Virginia, Patrick, Rosalie and Joseph. John and Mary had two sons: John and Michael. Mike and Francis had three girls: Virginia, Michele and Janet. Ben and Sylvia had four children: Andrew, who was hospitalized at a very early age, and was confined for the rest of his life, Elizabeth, Thomas, and Katherine ("Katie"); Charlie and Doreen had two children: Jeff and a daughter Stacey, who was killed in a boat accident in her teens. Grace's sister Ann and husband Al Cenigilio had three children: Jeanne, Alan and Jimmy. Mary and Gerald Johnston had three girls: Patricia, Maureen, and Joan. Gerald passed away when the girls were in their teens. Rose and George Caruana had five children: William, Christopher, Barbara, Roberta and Virginia. Both Rose and George have passed away.

Grace's mother died in 1950. Grace tells stories of her mother's skill in homemaking, her ability to make beautiful crocheted items with only string and wire and her kindness to people of all races. One of her mother's favorite sayings was "God made flowers of all colors in His garden".

After Virginia's death, Clement married Luigiana, a nice woman from Italy. When Clement died in 1968, Luigiana returned to Italy.

Many holidays during our marriage were spent in Ozone Park with other Deliso family members joining us. It was not unusual to have more than 20 people in attendance. Rose and George continued the traditions for some time after Grace's father died and Luigiana went back to Italy.

Rose's husband George bought a modest bungalow in Southampton, New York from his uncle (always known as "Uncle the Priest"). Though Southampton is often considered a very posh area, Towd Point was a sandy spit of land with tiny houses serving as second homes to firemen, policemen and other blue collar families from Queens and Brooklyn. The Caruana house had two small bedrooms, a half bath, an outdoor shower and an unfinished attic. Family members and guests were always welcome and crowding only added to the fun (at least for the children).

Possibly Grace will write her own biography and fill this section out.

Grace was the seventh child in her family, with only Rose and Mary younger. Of the four girls, she was the only one of them actively involved in the family business, acting as bookkeeper and secretary for her father.

Grace had attended Brooklyn High school for Girls, graduating in 1942, and entered NYU School of Education. She majored in education. In her senior year she was a student teacher in Brooklyn. After graduation from NYU, she got a job in Berriman Junior High School in East New York, a section of Brooklyn, teaching Home Economics. She continued with graduate courses.

In 1946, she had the "misfortune" of running into one Michael J. Ferrara. Her "misfortune" was the best thing that ever happened to me. She fully supported me in all my endeavors, took on the primary responsibility for the raising of our daughters. She put aside her course of professional life and took on and did an outstanding job as a mother and wife.

I could have accomplished nothing if she hadn't been at my side, and sometimes in front of me.

CHAPTER TWENTY

Ferrara Family

Jerry Ferrara—Brother

As I mentioned in an earlier segment, my brother's name was Gennaro, but he was known as Jerry to most people and Sonny to the family. In April 1942, he married his high school sweetheart, Josephine Cassucio. Their first child, Mary Anne, was born in April 1943. Jerry went into the Army in June 1943, assigned to the Signal Corps, for which he had been studying in New York for a year. I don't remember where he served, exactly, only that he was in the Pacific theater, moving from island to island, ending up with the MacArthur delegation at the surrender of Japan.

In November or December of 1945, he was honorably discharged as a Staff Sergeant, and went back to work as a tool and dye maker. July 1, 1949 he bought his first service station in Union City, with a small bank loan and some money he had saved.

On the 23rd of July 1949 Grace and I were married and he had to take a Saturday off to be my Best Man. It was at this location he met Ginger and Eleanor Schwartz who lived next door to the station. This friendship grew in intensity and lasted the full life of both of them with Ginger until he died and Eleanor living into her 90's dying in 2001. Both of them very early in the relationship became Uncle Ginger and Aunt Eleanor to all of us.

Over the years, Jerry and Josephine added more girls to the family: Geraldine, Patty, Christine, Eleanor and Francine.

At first, Jerry and Jo lived in an apartment around the corner from our family home on 34th street. This proved very convenient, especially for seeing the grandchildren. It also was convenient for me to use their "fancy" shower, a treat until I got married and bought our house in Bergenfield.

In April 1952, while Josephine was in the hospital giving birth to Christine, Jerry bought their house on Van Buren Avenue in Teaneck. They raised their family in this house with many fine parties and holidays until Jerry died on July 16 2000. Josephine lived in the house until moving to an assisted living center in 2004. Geraldine married Danny Wondrack and bought a house across the street. Their children Jennifer and Brian were lucky to live so close to their grandparents.

From his first day in the gasoline business, Jerry was actively involved in a trade organization of service station dealers, the New Jersey Gasoline Retailers Association. At one time, he had five or six different stations, but even so, he increased his activities for the Association.

He became the Executive Director of the organization consisting of over 2000 members. He was the main force behind the adoption of a Franchise Law in New Jersey, which provided some protection to individual dealers, from the arbitrary actions of the oil companies. He successfully prevented the oil companies attempt to introduce "self serve" gas purchases in N.J. which continues to be the only state with Oregon with the same prohibition. His drive took him to Congressional hearings to encourage the adoption of a National Petroleum Act for the benefit of gas dealers around the country.

As my brother got more involved with the Association, the state and national conventions became important functions. The state conventions were originally held in Atlantic City, which soon became too expensive for the members. Jerry arranged for the convention to be held at The Fallsview Hotel in the Catskills. The Association would take over the whole hotel with swimming, golf, tennis, boating, and nightclub entertainment every night, at a reasonable price. It was held there annually for 20 years. Each year's convention had a different theme for the main dinner and everyone had to participate, such as Roman night, Western night, and 4th of July.

The convention's business included a report by Jerry, adoption of major resolutions on issues confronted by the industry, a report by me on the legal problems and election of officers. We were finished by noon time each day. This allowed for true family vacations, with special arrangements for all ages.

The National conventions of the dealers as well as those of UNICO were held around the country and provided an excuse to have a family vacation.

In many years, the National UNICO conventions were held the week before or after the Dealers. In those instances, I was able to attend both conventions, though they were in opposite ends of the country: UNICO in Santa Monica, California and Dealers in Disney World in Florida; UNICO in New Orleans and Dealers in upper Minnesota; Dealers in New Orleans and UNICO in Milwaukee; Dealers in Washington D.C and UNICO in Kansas.

During his tenure, Jerry increased the financial strength of the New Jersey organization allowing it to own an office building in Springfield, New Jersey, to provide scholarships to children of Dealers, and to conduct business seminars and technical training programs.

Educating both the public and the state legislators, he was able to prove that self-service gas stations were not in the best interest of consumers, showing that the price of gasoline with full service was less than the self-service prices of adjoining states. Full service was also less hazardous with the potential of customers smoking while at the pumps and served the elderly and handicapped as well.

Now that he has died, it has been suggested that the oil companies will prevail and New Jersey will be the last state in the country to allow self service stations.

During all of his activities, Jerry found time to be Finance Chairman of the Trustees of St. Joseph's Church in Bogota. He became part of a team from the Archdiocese of Newark who advocated tithing in different parishes in the metropolitan area.

His dedication to his family, religion and business only slightly exceeded the enthusiasm he had for the New York Giants football team. He had nine tickets for all home games for many years and attended them with his daughter Maryanne and his nephew, Joe Shotino. The preferred means of transportation was an RV.

On game days, the crew was at the stadium by 11:30 AM, to enjoy a full breakfast. For the first game of the season, Josephine would cut a large watermelon in the shape of Giant stadium, with the pits representing fans and players. This was tricky work, but in keeping with the spirit of tailgating parties in the stadium parking lot. Around the lot were vehicles with fountains of flowing champagne, elaborate barbeques and service by short-skirted waitresses. Miss New Jersey was in attendance on one occasion.

After the tailgate party, it was into the stadium. Jerry's seats were in the top two rows on the 50-yard line. His seats were surrounded by those owned by his friends and colleagues. The end of the game didn't end the day. After the game, the party continued with a barbeque of sausage, peppers, hamburgers, steaks and all the trimmings.

When the Giants made the Super Bowl, he made the trip to California, but I don't know who won the Championship.

At his retirement dinner, New Jersey Governor Brendan Byrne, a personal friend of my brother, was the guest speaker.

Helen Cerrato—Sister

As I mentioned in an earlier chapter, my sister Helen's job as a legal secretary to Alfred Cozzi played an important role in my political life. Judge Cozzi was one of a few Republicans in Hudson County. When asked by the party in 1946 to find two County committee persons for our District, he asked his young secretary, Helen. She agreed even though she played the organ for a St. Anthony novena every Tuesday, and elections are held on Tuesdays providing I agreed to become the second person. We may have had a dozen Republican votes in the district, with six of them from my family.

Helen did not regret the fact that her playing interfered with her political career, for it was while playing that she met her husband, Gerry Cerrato who sang in St. Rocco's choir. They were pillars of the church. Gerry was one of the first deacons of the Newark Archdiocese. Both remained active in the choir and other functions of the church for the rest of their lives.

At some point, a young girl by the name of Dora Sharpe became a member of the choir. Dora's family life was unsettled, to say the least, and Helen and Jerry offered her a place in their home. They urged her to continue her education. She heeded this advice, graduating from the nursing program of Felician College in Lodi. She became Director of Nursing at the infirmary for retired nuns at Felician College, where she remained until June 2003. With her ever present camera and cheerful manner, Dora remains a good friend to our family to this day.

Ida Ferrara—Sister

My sister Ida never married and cared for our younger brother until his death in 1952 and my mother until her death on January 31, 1962. Forced to leave school early, she worked in garment factories sewing dresses, formal evening gowns and ladies' suits until she retired. When my sister Virginia married and moved to a two-family house in Bergenfield, Ida and my mother moved there as well. Like Helen, she remained active in St Rocco's Church and later in St. John's in Bergenfield.

Virginia Pannuzzo—Twin Sister

Virginia was my twin sister, who died in 1968. She was a blonde, with a pale complexion compared to my darker skin. She married George Pannuzzo, an electrician who eventually had his own business. His business grew with the extensive housing construction that took place in Bergen County. During her life Virginia helped make ends meet, becoming an active sales person for cosmetics, pottery, dishes, silverware and other goods.

They had four children: Michael, Joanne, Gary, and Ronald. Michael joined his father's business and expanded it significantly, operating it from his home in Bergenfield. Michael married a woman named Sigred, and they had two children. Their son became a star basketball player from Bergen Catholic High School in Oradell, earning a scholarship to St. Michael's University in New Hampshire. Upon graduation, he was employed by Merrill Lynch. They also have a daughter.

Virginia and George's second child was Joanne. Joanne was employed part time as a bookkeeper and later, a travel agent, but her real avocation is hot air ballooning. She earned her license and bought her own balloon. In 2005, her longtime partner, Jacques Deveroy, succumbed to colon cancer.

Gary chose Wall Street and is a commodity trader. He is married with several children. Ronald became an architect. After attending school in New Mexico, he remained there and married.

CHAPTER TWENTY-ONE

VACATIONS

Probably our first vacation was in 1958, a motor trip to Massachusetts visiting Grace's brothers in Worcester, Springfield, and Cape Cod. Then in 1961, my UNICO activities justified a month long motor trip to a convention in Houston, Texas. We drove down the Appalachian Highway through Virginia, Tennessee, to New Orleans.

From there we went to San Antonio into Mexico. After the convention in Houston, our return took us through Oklahoma then Missouri where we met President Truman at his library. From there we traveled through Illinois to Lincoln's home town.

Subsequent UNICO activities provided excuses for a summer vacations: Miami Florida (providing a side trip to Jamaica); Washington, DC, (providing a side trip to Williamsburg); Milwaukee providing a side trip to Canada; and trips to Boston, and Las Vegas.

Our family has always enjoyed vacations. One should be entitled "Granddaughter Brigitte's First Trip to Europe in Person". (Previously, she traveled inutero with her parents Donna and Ray to Scandinavia and Russia).

London-Scotland-Ireland

Donna was the motivating force behind this vacation: she was to speak at a conference of lawyers in London. Grace and I thought a return to London would be interesting. When we got into the planning, it was clear that we had a more important destination. While we would visit London and Edinburgh, the main focus of the trip would be Ireland.

We were fortunate to have a private tour of Lloyds of London. We had an opportunity to be on the floor of the exchange, which has members who arrange for major insurance policies around the world. It originally was set up to insure cargo ships traveling the sea.

Buckingham Palace

London's Tower Bridge

From London we took the train along the coast of England and Scotland to Edinborough and visited St. Andrew Golf Course. Reservations are required one year in advance to play this course.

Famous 18th Hole on Old Course

Swilken or Standbridge

Brigitte was to visit the birth place of her father and her Aunt Ann – not to mention her Grandfather Simon and Grandmother Betty. We found the house where Simon lived, the school he attended and St. Peters Church where Simon and Betty were married and Raymond and Anne were baptized.

Mt. Tremblant

A few years earlier (2000), Donna had come up with a similar "excuse" for us to join them on vacation. The convention of the same lawyers group was held at Mt. Tremblant in Canada. We added a tour of Montreal and enjoyed the popular ski resort, which was also a fine summer vacation area.

Eastern Canada

Brigitte is a favorite companion for us on vacation. She came with us on a trip to eastern Canada, including Halifax, Prince Edward's Island and the Maritimes. Some of the highlights of the tour were a boat trip to view the whale birthplaces, a visit to the House of Green Gables on St. Edward Island, and the famous Bay of Fundy where the tide changes a minimum of 25 feet every 12 hours.

Brigitte at Wheel

Whale

Bay of Fundy

Oh, and Brigitte's parents were with us, too, taking care of things like airline tickets, hotels, van rental, food and other trivia.

Donna and Raymond drove a van, equipped with personal video and audio; Brigitte, Grace and I enjoyed terrific scenery, historical sites, wonderful swimming pools, excellent French fries and a true Canadian delight—Cow's Homemade Ice Cream.

Australia-New Zealand

In 1991, we took a trip to Australia and New Zealand, again with Donna and Raymond. We flew first class on a two story 747 using thousands of Donna's frequent flyer miles and a (relatively) small cash contribution

We flew from Kennedy Airport to San Francisco where we spent two days and one night. We flew five hours from San Francisco with a stop in Hawaii, and then eight hours to Auckland, New Zealand, called the City of Sails.

We started in Auckland, visited the Newman Club, and took a boat tour of the city, with a tour of the city of Devonport which is the residence of many people working in Auckland. It was a beautiful clean city and a Naval Base, with extensive beaches. There are 69 volcano hills surrounding the city.

We arrived at the Rotorua Hotel where we had a special Mauri (Australia's native people) dinner and saw a Mauri dancing and concert show.

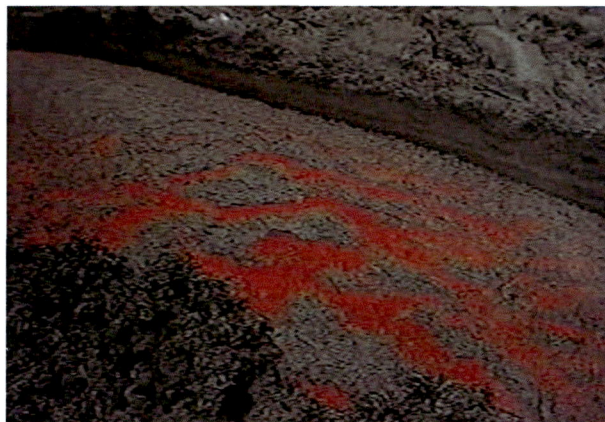

We then arranged a tour with a guide named Michael. The whole Rotorua area is covered with bubbling geysers and volcano country, and colorful steaming sulfur lakes. The natives displayed their extensive skill in wood carving of all kinds, and the training of sheep dogs. We had a Mauri barbeque and an explanation of Maori customs including rubbing noses for friendship.

We continued the tour and at one point the signs warned visitors not descend the steps to see the full effect of the Wairoa Falls. The notice was very accurate as we learned when I insisted on going down, much to Graces chagrin.

Then we flew to Sidney, toured that city with its famous Opera House at a cost of $102 million and completed in 1973. We had the opportunity to visit and ride around the famous New South Wales Country Club located on the ocean similar to Pebble Beach Country Club in California.

Next, we flew to Canberra, capital of Australia. There was a major dispute as to whether the capital should be Sidney or Melbourne. To resolve the argument, they compromised on Canberra and created this new city. Having carefully planned our trip to coincide with Australia Day on January 26th (all right, it was an accident), we were welcomed by fireworks and barbeques. The friendly Aussies happily offered food and drink to a wandering American with a video camera.

While Donna and Ray slept late one morning, Grace and I decided to watch the hot air balloon flights. By luck, there was an empty place on one of the balloons and I was asked along. I got great footage of the beautifully planned city of Canberra, with its lakes and hills.

The next stop was Tasmania. From our base in Hobart, we traveled up Mount Wellington then off to Port Arthur, where we visited the ruins of the penal settlement. The site is the most popular tourist attraction in Tasmania, although it is probably best known for the massacre of thirty five people in 1996, the worst "killing spree" of all time.

Australia is a large country and from the wooded hills of Tasmania, we flew to the tropical beaches and rain forest of North Queensland. From Cairns, we took a hydrofoil out to the Great Barrier Reef. On the reef, there was an area in which swimming, snorkeling and scuba diving was permitted, with all necessary equipment provided. Donna and Raymond took advantage of the snorkeling. Grace and I rode in a glass-sided submarine, which traveled in a large, slow circle among the beautiful fish and reef life.

To cap our trip, we stayed at the Park Hyatt Hotel in Sydney. Nestled under the famous Sydney Harbor Bridge, with a stunning view of the city skyline, the Opera House and the Botanical Gardens, this hotel is a favorite with visiting celebrities. Our rooms, we were told, were on the floor which had been used by Frank Sinatra in his last trip to Australia.

Tauck Austria

While I am talking about vacations I recall a Tauck tour of Austria, Switzerland and Germany in July 1994. It was 13 days starting with a flight to Vienna. We took a two day tour of Austria. The second day we toured the sights of Vienna including a memorable concert in the park and beautiful residents dancing the waltz at Schounbraun Palace.

From Vienna we went to Salzburg and ate in and toured Mozart's house. We traveled to the town of Monzasse, and viewed the church famous for the wedding of Julie Andrews and Christopher Plummer in the *Sound of Music*.

We then went to Munich and enjoyed a sumptuous dinner which lasted four hours in the same hotel we stayed for the night. We also visited the Palace of Ludwig and the extensive gardens with statues etc., and the Glockenspiel with revolving mannequins built into a tower in the square.

We traveled to the French province of Alsace Lorain. There we boarded a ship holding 80 passengers (40 from our group) to go up the Rhine River, which required traversing several locks. We stopped at the town of Spire for a tour then onto viewing a cathedral in Heidelberg, Germany, which was known as a college or university town. We had an interesting visit to the outdoor stage area for the performance of the Festival of Heidelberg.

Heading up the Rhine to Cologne, we enjoyed beautiful views of the many castles on the Rhine. In the early days the owners would extract a fee from the boats. With the story of Laura Lie statue who would entice the sailors to come to the shore and crash their ships. The famous Cologne Cathedral took 600 years to be built.

Mediterranean

We took a Mediterranean cruise with Eddy and Betty Garino from September 30 through October 15, 2000. We flew to Venice where we boarded a Renaissance Cruise ship, which would be our hotel for the entire trip to Barcelona.

In Venice, we had a tour of St. Mark's Square, and then took a trip to the island of Murano famous for its crystal. We were taken to a factory and shown the "art" of glass blowing, then continued the boat ride to the island of Barano famous for its lace.

The first stop was Croatia, then to the Isle of Corfu in Greece, Sicily, Rome, Malta, Naples, Florence, Siena, Lucca, Pisa Corsica (home of Napoleon), Nice, Monaco (Cathedral where Princess Grace is buried), Marseille, Palm de Mallorca (Mallorca pearls), and Barcelona.

ST MARKS

THE

MT ETNA

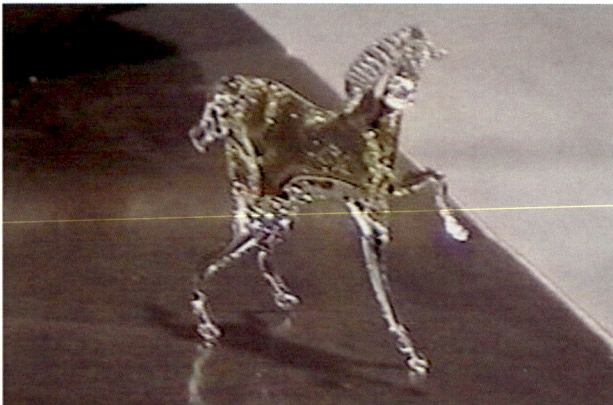
Murano Blown Glass

PRINCESS GRACE TOMB

Mallorca Pearls

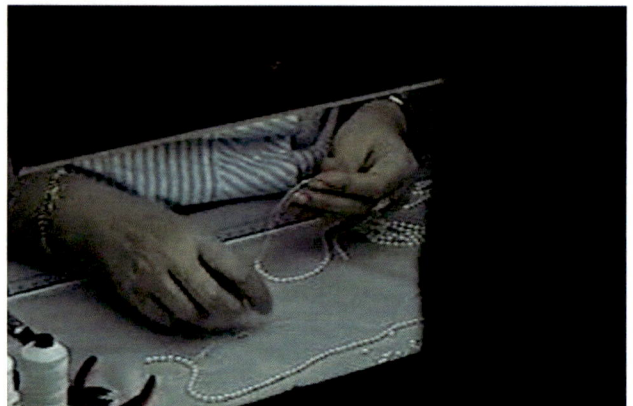
Mallorca Pearls

Alaska

Our 17 day trip to Alaska in August 1993 began with a flight to Seattle and a bus trip to Vancouver. We then had a seven day bus tour of Western Canada, viewing the beautiful Minter Gardens, We took a special bus to the top of the glacier about eight miles from the main road. The guide was giving all of us Scotch with fresh water running through the glacier.

We reached Lake Louise and stayed at the 1,000 plus room Chateau Lake Louise Hotel owned by the Canadian Pacific Railroad.

We then went to Bath. We took a helicopter ride to view an outstanding picture of some of the glaciers from the top. This portion of the trip ended in the large Stanley Park in Vancouver.

We boarded our ship for the seven day trip to Anchorage. The first stop was Ketchecan where we took a twin-engine 10 passenger pontoon plane for a view of the port and landed in the middle of a large lake. We got off the plane and stood on the pontoons for picture taking of the surrounding mountains. Then onto the Magnificent Mendenhall glacier which is actively running from Juneau. The icebergs are 100 feet deep and 200 feet above water.

When we reached Skagway, we took a single engine 4-seater plane ride over the glaciers, to view crevices 100 or more feet deep.

After this trip we took the White Pass Railroad single track ride up and thru the mountain, which showed the trail that supposedly was used by the gold rush travelers, and reaches about a ¼ mile into Canada. We then traveled the inner passage to Glacier Bay and viewed portions of the glacier breaking off into the bay.

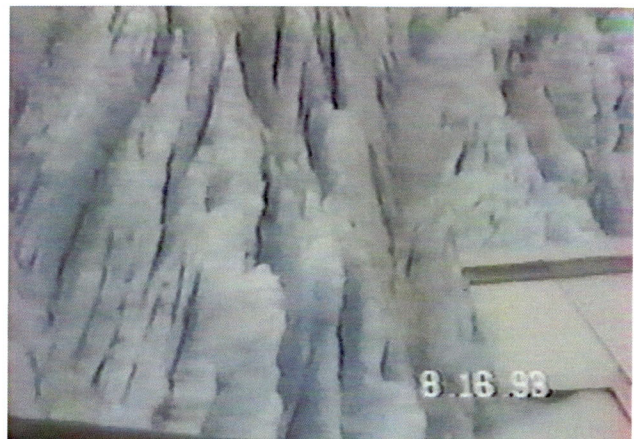

In Anchorage we boarded a domed train for a three day trip to Mt Mc Kinley, where I took another helicopter ride with phenomenal views of Glacier Mountains, and visited the site of a training camp for the dogs used on the Itinerod. We then took a 12 passenger high speed motor boat up the river to see actual camp sites used by hunters in winters and summers.

The sites are more than nine miles to the nearest road, and 150 miles from the nearest grocery store and were originally used for persons looking for a gold strain. There were several different guides explaining all of the living conditions.

We then boarded the train heading to Fairbanks where we took a river cruise and passed a location used by President Nixon on a return trip from China where he had a 45 minute meeting with Pope John XXIII. We stopped at another dog training camp used by Susan Butcher, a four time Iditarod winner in 1986, 1987, 1988 and 1990. We then were given a tour of the Trans-Alaska Pipe Line explaining the construction and maintenance of the pipe line.

We took a plane back to Denver with a short layover (where the Pope was visiting), and then on to Newark.

Panama Canal

On our trip through the Panama Canal from October 8 to 20, 1999, we were fortunate to get a first class cabin on Crystal Cruise Line's Harmony, for a reasonable fee, as Lisa was working as a craft teacher with her friend Marj Gerstle. We flew from Ft. Lauderdale to Cancun Mexico. We met Marj on the ship and visited Costa Rica.

The next day we entered the Panama Canal from the Pacific side. The first series of locks are about 100 feet wide and requires a lift of 85 feet. After passing thru man-made Lake Gatun, the ship is lowered the 85 feet to the Caribbean side, at Cartagena, Columbia. It takes a full day to travel through the canal.

The next stop was the Cayman Islands, then onto Cozumel, Mexico where Grace bought some jewelry. The next stops were New Orleans, Carnival's Mardi-Gras Warehouse, the French Quarter, and, Antoine's Restaurant.

Caribbean—Albi

In February 2005 we took a Caribbean cruise with our Albi friends, for a period of 13 days, leaving from Ft. Lauderdale to Margarita, Curacao, Barbadoes, Domenica, St. Thomas and Princess Cay, a private island in the Cayman Island group.

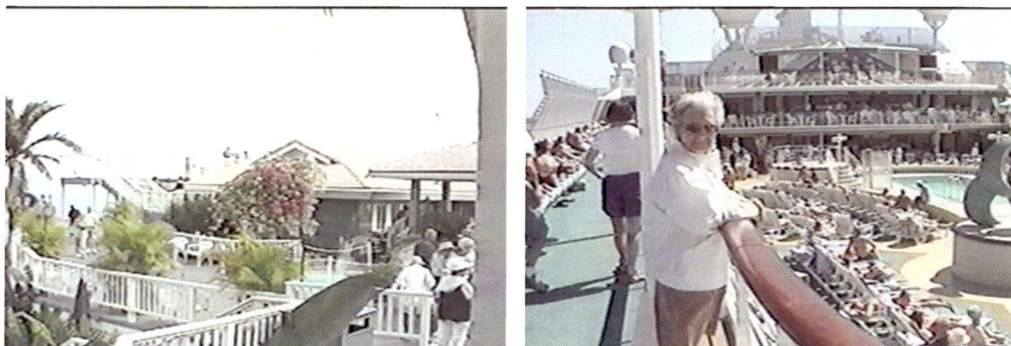

The Great House, St. Thomas

The Albi Group

Las Vegas

In August 2000 we took a trip to Las Vegas after UNICO convention in California, staying at the outstanding Venetian Hotel. The duplicating of the Grand Canal and gondoliers, and the street singing and shops were superb.

The exterior of the many casinos were breathtaking with the waterfalls, and architecture. This was seen while looking at Caesar's lobby and "indoor street scene" with singing operatic music and enormous statues. MGM lobby and the "EFX" show, the dragon and fire show, the Bellagio Lobby and the Cirque du Soleil acrobatic show, Paris with the Arc de Triomphe and the Eifffel Tower, New York with a replica of the streets of the city, including the bowery, Greenwich Village, China Town, and the Statue of Liberty.

Hawaii

In 1967 I was sworn in as National President of UNICO in Santa Monica and arranged for an additional vacation to Hawaii with the children. We were set up in a luxurious hotel with the ocean on one side and a golf course on the other. We took a bus tour visiting the Dole farms, and a rain forest.

Another day we took a boat to the Island of Maui with its beautiful gardens, and the site of a volcano eruption.

Sicily—Corradino

Our visit, in April 1997, to Sicily was arranged by Mike Corradino, to visit the birth place of his parents and also of his wife Anna Belle. There were only 14 people and were met at the Rome airport by a guide and a private bus We traveled Naples with our first stop the town of Pompeii with a tour guide explanation of the destruction caused by the eruption of nearby Mt. Vesuvius.

We took a boat over to Capri. While there we took a small craft to visit the famous Blue Grotto, and tour the island. We were nearly stranded there when a storm rose with such fury, there was concern as to whether or not the craft could withstand the sea. We were fortunate to be the last craft back, with a wild churning sea.

Pompeii

The next day we crossed the Meditterrean to Messina, Scily with our destination Taormina, and Mt. Etna.

The trip continued around the island to Siracusa with a tour of the Greek Temples and ruins there.

We then went north to the primary objective of this trip: to visit Geraci, the birth places of Anna Belle and Mike Corradino's fathers. We also visited the local Chapel of St. Anna which Mike Corradino and other Passaic and Clifton Unicans provided funds for restoration of the historical site.

Our return was to Palermo with a city tour and then the plane back to direct to Newark.

Entrance to the Blue Grotto

CHAPTER TWENTY-TWO

Columbians

I became involved with an organization known as the Columbians in the early 1980s. It is an Italian-American group whose purpose is to foster the image of Americans of Italian descent. It was not to be a fraternal club with life insurance programs or clubhouses as such. It was intended to be more a service club like UNICO or the Lions or Rotary Clubs but without national affiliation. It would embark on active charities, scholarships, hardships of individuals, and other cultural endeavors. Some of the early members thinking it would be patterned along the line of the Columbian organization in New York, but with an emphasis on Northern New Jersey, and without a building.

John Ingannamorte, Paul Petrillo, Frank Buono, Gene DePaola, Gerry Cardinale and I were part of the original organizers. It was intended to be a select group of people in the "Italian" community who could foster the ideals expressed. John became the first President and I think Paul became the Secretary with the other officers filled by persons recruited. Joe Setteneri, who was a retired businessman, became actively involved in the functions held, the fund raising, etc.

Paul Patti I believe was also one of the original members, and in later years became an active "behind the scenes" member but intricately involved in raising major funds through publication of an ad journal connected with the Annual Christmas Party. This function and a golf outing in the spring provided the major funds enabling the granting of 40 to $50,000 to various causes.

Charlie Volpe became a subsequent President and introduced a new member by the name of Arthur Stanton. Together they continued the raising of substantial dollars for the organization.

At the moment I will not set forth all of the persons who held the office of President, but only to say each of them contributed to the growth of the organization in various ways and continued the organization's ability to donate $50,000 to $70,000 every year to the charities selected by the group.

CHAPTER TWENTY-THREE

UNICO

Around 1956, I had become involved in an Italian-American organization (or as I prefer saying), an American organization of Italian descent) called UNICO. This proved to be the beginning of a major part of my life. UNICO means "one" or "unique". The pillars of the organization are Unity, Neighborliness, Integrity, Charity, and Opportunity.

My first experience with UNICO was in 1947 or 1948. Grace was asked to be the Confirmation sponsor of her niece, Virginia Deliso, daughter of her oldest brother Joe. During our visit, the Springfield chapter of UNICO had a family picnic. Joe was an active, charter member of the group. In one of the organized games at the picnic, I won a shoeshine kit and an electric shoe brush (which still functions). It's possible that Grace's brother, not too certain of my chances of professional success, made sure I had a shoe shine stand to fall back on to support his sister. I hope my story proves his concern unfounded.

UNICO grew during the 1950's. Mike Corradino of the Passaic Chapter learned that his former pastor at St. Anthony Church, Father Henry D'Angelis, had been transferred to St. Francis Parish in Hackensack. Mike tapped him for help in setting up a new chapter. Sal Corradino, Mike's cousin, a salesman in paper bags and supplies, knew a considerable number of Italian-American businessmen who were eligible for membership. Gus LaCorte and Joe Salerno, also from the Passaic chapter, joined Mike in forming the Hackensack chapter. Chartered in 1956, I became a Vice President in the organization and in two years became Chapter President.

UNICO became an important part of our life. I moved through District and National offices to become National President in 1966. I continue my participation to this day.

From 1958 through the nineties, I attended national conventions all over the USA. The conventions usually took place at the end of July or beginning of August, a perfect time for a family vacation. Our vacations were at least three weeks to a month.

A Texas convention was an excuse to visit Mexico. From Florida in 1964, we hopped over for a quick visit to Jamaica. Following a California convention, we flew to Hawaii. Even Milwaukee served as a gateway to Canada, with our daughter Lisa and niece Barbara Caruana.

Others were held in New Orleans, Las Vegas, Chicago, Boston, Washington DC, with side trips to Williamsburg and Philadelphia.

In 1965, the UNICO national convention was held at the newly opened Chalfonte-Hadden Hall Hotel in Atlantic City. The Saturday formal banquet was over-sold with close to 1100 people. (The chairman of the convention, Joe Salerno had planned with meticulous detail during the prior year.)

The banquet had its share of issues. The main ballroom was brand new and there was some question if it would be ready for an August convention. The keynote speaker and honoree was Pennsylvania Supreme Court Justice Michael Musmanno. Unfortunately, he spoke for close to an hour. The general tedium was relieved when a bat flew in through a window near the ceiling of the room. You can imagine our anxiety (especially that of the ladies with their hairdos), as the bat searched for a way out, fortunately, it found an open window and escaped.

My most memorable UNICO moment was installation as National President in Santa Monica, California in 1966, as I was sworn in by my friend, Mike Corradino. A close second, though, followed the UNICO convention in Houston, Texas in 1961. On the way home, we had driven through Missouri. In Kansas City, we had the honor and pleasure of a private meeting with President Harry Truman at his library.

At that point, the girls were 11, 8, and 5. President Truman told us about his daughter Margaret, then performing in a play in New Jersey. "Give 'em hell, Harry" offered a few critical comments about a well-known New York journalist who didn't say nice

Grace, Donna, Virginia, Lisa, Truman Secy, MJF President Truman

things about his daughter's performance. Interestingly, the play was taking place at a small regional theater in the Bergen Mall in Paramus—practically in our backyard.

A few weeks later, President Truman visited the playhouse. As was his custom, he walked around the center greeting people, an event that received full press coverage. The New York Daily News had a front page picture of his walk, which encouraged my children to show their picture with "Daddy's friend" in his library.

During my term as National President of UNICO, in November 1966, Florence, Italy suffered a major flood. This became a major project for me. We organized an aid program and raised $500,000 in cash and supplies. In later years, UNICO officers visited Florence to view the improvements our aid had helped make possible.

On one of my visits to Kansas City, I was "kidding" Dr. Di Renna about his profession. In response he offered me a chance to view one of his surgeries. I jumped at the offer even though it required my being at the hospital at 7:00 AM the next day. When I arrived at the operating room area I was greeted by one of the nurses and instructed to take off my jacket, shirt and shoes. I was given a blue robe, slippers for my feet, and a mask and cover for my head.

When I entered the operating room the woman patient was already prepared for surgery, which was to remove a tumor in her abdomen. I had difficulty watching the initial cutting of the skin to the extent of approximately two to three inches (the woman was quite obese). The sides of the opening were held apart by "vice type" equipment. There were four to five nurses assisting, along with an anesthesiologist.

I was permitted to look into the opening and view the removal of a small foot ball size tumor, with the doctor examining other organs in the area. The tumor was taken to be examined and the nurses proceeded to sew up the opening. In the "usual" way there was a count for the sponges which were used, and Dr Di Renna said there was one missing. A few nurses' faces lit up with concern until the Doctor showed them one he had hidden and was only teasing them.

Friendships formed in UNICO have lasted through the years. Mike Corradino, still active in his Passaic-Clifton chapter, at 91 years of age, is on my e-mail list. We were traveling companions on a trip to Sicily in 1997; an adventure Grace and I, (and 11 others), enjoyed very much. Mike planned the entire trip, including a visit to the village which was the home town of both his and his wife Anna Belle's fathers.

Joe Salerno became General Counsel for UNICO. A close confidant for many years, Joe was my roommate at the National meetings we attended without our families. Later, he was appointed a Superior Court Judge in Passaic County. Gus La Corte, owner and publisher of a weekly newspaper in Passaic County, served as National President of UNICO. He was one of my advisors and supporters as I climbed up the National chairs to the Presidency. Both Joe and his wife Connie, and Gus and his wife Sarah have passed on to greater rewards, though they are warmly remembered by Grace and me.

Our children became friends with other Unican children with whom they shared some of the escapades of the conventions. Between conventions, UNICO activity required many meetings and social gatherings.

During this same period, my political involvement began. Dinners and dances, many black tie affairs, began to fill our schedule. Always a trooper, Grace nevertheless asserted herself — she was not going to sit at a table all night while I "worked the room". As a result, we formed a small group of Unicans to take dancing lessons every two weeks. We rotated homes with a traveling teacher with a little record player. The pressure was on; if any one didn't practice and held up the class – watch out for trouble.

Often I would come home from the office and grab Grace to try a few steps, as she was trying to prepare supper. Our children would witness these machinations.

Through the years, our UNICO connections continue. Two days after Christmas in 2001, Grace had some neighbors in for tea and dessert. We learned that Joan Martini's father-in-law was Phil Martini, the patriarch of Passaic UNICO. Her husband, Mike, has been active in our

Spring Meadow organization, including a term as President. We have become good friends in New Jersey as well as in Florida.

Another charter member of Hackensack UNICO was Al Garino, owner of a very large roofing company. His son and grandsons have followed in the business, benefitting from Al's guidance. In 1973, his brother Ed and I became members of Ridgewood Country Club. We regularly play golf together there and in Florida.

Angelo Ferreri, another charter member, was a pharmaceutical salesman. In his travels, he visited Milwaukee and met Dr. Ed Leone. During a conversation, they realized they both knew me. Ed was a grade and high school friend from Union City. His brother's father–in-law was the doctor who delivered my twin sister and me in 1922. Ed became an active member of Milwaukee UNICO. As a sideline, he became a Professional Parliamentarian.

Ignatious Belgiovine became a member of the Hackensack Chapter in 1958. In 1966, he became Chapter President. Also in 1958, he bought a tailoring business in Hackensack, working in it until 2000. Moving to Maywood in 1962, he was active in Maywood organizations becoming President of the Rotary, Commander of the American Legion. He and his wife Mella also worked in Queen of Peace church and school activities. Mella was a charter member of the Ladies of Hackensack UNICO.

Domemic Albi, whose brother Mario was a Past National President of UNICO, and Serena, his wife, live near our apartment in Florida and we visit regularly with them. Mario spent February and March 2002 with them and we enjoyed our visit with him.

Joe D'Elia was yet another charter member of Hackensack UNICO. He owned, with his father, the Queen Anne Restaurant in Teaneck, where we held our monthly meetings and dinners. I spent many nights after meetings, sitting in his office or the kitchen, talking about families and our desire for a successful life.

We might not have realized it then, but real success depended upon our wives and children. Without their support, we couldn't have enjoyed our participation in business and social events. They paid the price, and we can only hope that it had proven to be of long-term benefit to them.

After selling the Queen Anne Restaurant, Joe bought the Innwood Manor in Teaneck, a substantial catering facility. His son, Ronnie went into the business and ran the day-to-day operation while Joe was tied up with the paper business.

Joe's father had been a partner in the Bruno & D'Elia waste paper business, which Joe took over when his father died. The company was sold to Garden State Paper, a national paper recycling business which converted waste paper to newsprint. He continued to run the business for the national company until his death.

He purchased some warehouse units in Hackensack and elsewhere, as well as residential properties in New Jersey and in Rockland County. His sons, Bill and Ronnie, continue to manage these properties for the family

Even with all these activities, Joe was at the restaurant almost every night. So was his wife, Josephine, helping out in the kitchen, on the floor or wherever else she was needed. Joe's sisters Helen, Nettie and Betty also did their time waitressing.

On the way to the restaurant one day, Joe and Josephine were in a head on head collission, Joe died on impact and Josephine suffered multiple injuries. It was a devastating loss, but the D'Elia family pulled together to take care of Josephine and the family's business.

CHAPTER TWENTY-FOUR

2001—PGA Tournament

In the winter of 2000, I received a call from Fred Nydegger, general chairman of the Senior PGA tournament, scheduled for Ridgewood Country Club in May 2001. This was the first time this tournament would be held outside Florida. Fred asked me to video the tournament, in my almost-official capacity of Ridgewood's Video Historian. I was delighted!

The first meeting to be recorded was a press conference in April 2000, which required me to leave Florida a little early. During the summer of 2000, many details had to be resolved. Though the club has a good-sized parking lot, it was inadequate for the number of cars expected. Parking would be provided at nearby Bergen County Community College and at not-so-nearby Sharpe Headquarters in Mahwah. From Mahwah, spectators would be bussed to the course. Traffic arrangements were coordinated with the Paramus and Bergen County Police departments. The course practice area would serve as primary storage for 250 automobiles, generators, corporate tents, the pro shop and other related services. Emergency medical arrangements were made with the Paramus EMS group and Valley Hospital.

In October 2000, another formal meeting was held. To maintain good relations, the club's neighbors were invited to a party where the details of the tournament were shared.

Throughout 2000 and 2001, preparations continued. The course was readied for the actual tournament and the rest of the grounds prepared for vendors, toilets, press facilities and equipment storage.

When I returned from Florida in May, 2001, I plunged into the real job of recording what was taking place: construction of grandstands, installation of corporate tents, creating the vendors' booths and kiosks and many other aspects.

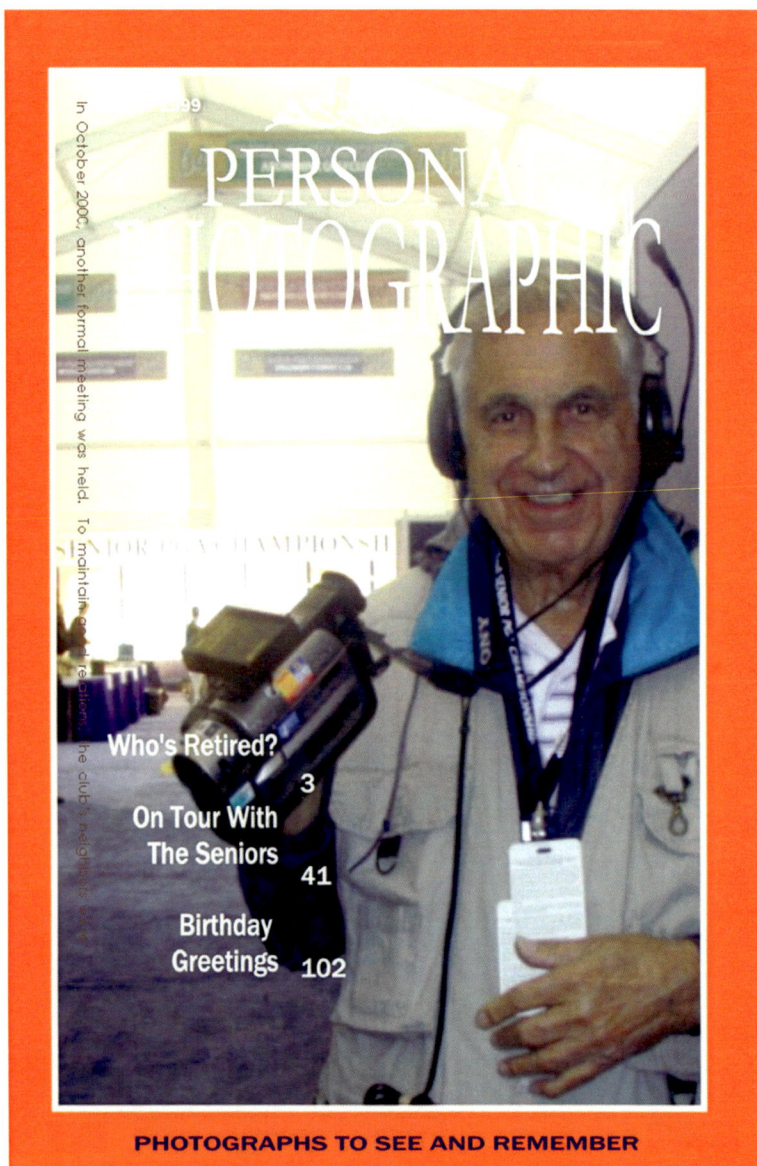

PERSONAL PHOTOGRAPHIC

Who's Retired? 3

On Tour With The Seniors 41

Birthday Greetings 102

PHOTOGRAPHS TO SEE AND REMEMBER

The tournament began on May 21st and ended on the 27th. The professionals started arriving on Monday the 22nd and were met by dreary weather. Monday through Saturday, there was real concern about how the weather would affect the tournament and the golf course. Personally, I worried about my ability to videotape the events. Rising to the challenge, I donned rain gear and slipped a plastic cover on my camera for seven full days of work. I shot about eight hours of tape interviews with Ridgewood members, and a fair amount of interviews of the pro golfers.

Jim Thorpe and PGA Official

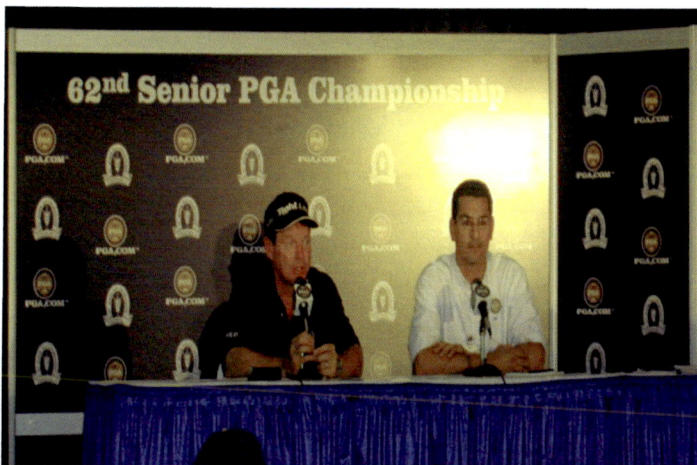

Tom Watson and PGA Official

Because I was producer, director and complete onsite camera crew, I taped 14 hours of commercial coverage as well.

From the end of the tournament until September I spent hours reviewing and editing tapes. I had to balance my desire to adequately record the historical events and the reality that I'd have to reduce it to a reasonable time or no one would watch it. After preparing multiple versions, I concluded that the balance was struck with a tape of one hour 17 minutes. The final product captures early meetings, preparation and construction, through the final hole where Tom Watson won by one stroke to the celebratory buffet for all members afterwards.

CHAPTER TWENTY-FIVE

2003—An Eventful Year

In February of 2003, while in Florida, I had begun experiencing shortness of breath, fatigue and swelling in my legs and ankles. All of this I blithely ignored, until, by March, even I had to admit there was a problem. I called my doctor up north for a recommendation and he did not have one, but said it was important to see a doctor.

On March 16, 2003, Paul Patti and I were going to play golf. Fortunately, Paul mentioned Dr. William George, an internist, who was formerly a neighbor of his brother Joe. I gave him a call, mentioned the Pattis and he agreed to see me the next day. (How often do you hear that possibility?). I told him that the only sign of my condition was difficulty breathing. He took an x-ray and a cardiogram. My lungs were filled with fluid. My legs were swollen from the ankles to above the knee and my heart beat was irregular. He said I had to go to the hospital emergency room.

I argued "You never saw me before and I never saw you before. I ain't going to the hospital. I deal in alternatives." Dr. George responded, "Mr. Ferrara you have an alternative. You can go out and play golf and have a blood clot and die."

You know he won. Fortunately Frank and Chris Buono were available to drive my car (Grace had little experience or desire to drive it) and to take Grace home. During my stay in the hospital Frank and Chris drove Grace back and forth. They advised the Albis with whom we were to have a St. Joseph celebration, and also were able to use two tickets at FAU for a Regis Philbin show the next night.

Dr. George called the emergency room, wrote instructions and called a cardiologist, Dr. Babik. Both were at the hospital that afternoon. After six days wired up with blood thinners and diuretics to remove the fluid in my lungs and legs, it was determined that I had atrial fibrillation. In simple terms, this means the pulsing of the left and right sides of my heart were no longer coordinated.

Despite my insistence to the contrary, Lisa flew down to help us. Completely ignoring my good natured (and not so good natured) grumbling, she was of enormous assistance, taking notes, asking questions and helping Grace through a difficult time.

Upon release from the hospital, I was monitored by Dr. George. He took many blood tests, blood pressure tests and reviewed all my medications and vitamins. His guidance and diagnosis were outstanding. No surgery was required.

When I returned to New Jersey in May, my doctors complimented the work of those in Florida. On August 13, 2003, my atrial fibrillation was shocked back to normal. While my condition is being monitored, I haven't had another episode.

Our adventures weren't over. In the middle of May, after we had returned to New Jersey, Grace went shopping in Paramus. As she drove through Midland Park, Grace's car was totaled by a young lady coming out of Burger King without looking. The other vehicle – a big SUV—pushed Grace's Taurus onto the lawn of a bank building, across the street. Grace suffered a bloody nose, friction burn on her face, and bumped her head on the visor. Her seat belt prevented more serious injuries, although the car was totally destroyed.

The second week of June, feeling recovered from the accident. Grace arranged to play her first golf game since the previous fall. During the game, Grace walked through some bushes to tell the caddy that the group behind her could go through. Her partner, driving the golf cart, went to pick her up and hit her in the left knee with the cart. The knee was cracked. Fortunately, no surgery was necessary. After therapy, it substantially healed.

Poor Grace's problems were not over. In the second week of July Grace experienced severe abdominal pains for several hours. Finally, at 9:00 PM, we called the ambulance for the trip to the emergency room of Valley Hospital. Our daughters quickly joined us there. After an all night vigil in the emergency room and a CAT scan, the doctors wanted to operate. Because they were unable to tell us what the actual problem was, we insisted on a second opinion and more information. After three more days of x-rays, tests and intravenous feeding, Grace was still in pain and still had some kind of obstruction. The doctors concluded surgery was necessary.

Although apprehensive, we agreed. Ultimately, we were told that Grace had suffered an intestinal hernia and an adhesion, which is unusual in a "virgin" stomach (that is, one which had never undergone surgery). She seems to have healed nicely, but she may not want to wear her bikini in Florida.

Reflecting on this chapter in our lives, I conclude that we have been blessed with good health and we continue to be blessed. My heart problems could have been far more serious and I could have needed surgery or died. The car that hit Grace's car could have hit the driver's door or turned the car over. Her knee could have been far more damaged. Her abdominal obstruction could have been a tumor.

Still, this has been a sobering experience and it certainly has made me reflect on my very fortunate life. It's also made me ease further into my retirement, such as it is.

CHAPTER TWENTY-SIX

Grace's 80th Birthday—Florida

In December 2003, while in Florida, I received a call from my son-in-law Joseph. He informed me that a decision had been made by the rest of our family during Thanksgiving dinner in Glen Rock. The entire family was coming to Florida in April. My initial question was: Why?—followed quickly by "Where would we put everyone?"

He advised me that our daughters wanted to celebrate Grace's 80th birthday with her. I asked why it couldn't wait until we got home. My questions were irrelevant. The decision was final. They would be there on Saturday, April 17th, Grace's birthday.

As Joseph explained, non-refundable airline reservations had been made. A complex series of hotel reservations were also in place, arranged to meet the family's various needs.

My mission, which I had to accept, was to scout possible locations for the celebration. I suggested either the social room in the building or across the street at the beach house. These were unacceptable to the New Jersey contingent; it had to be a special place, like the Breakers Hotel in Palm Beach or La Maison Vielle, an elegant restaurant in Boca Raton.

The central event evolved from Saturday night dinner for the 11 immediate family members to a party with 30 or 40 of our friends. Saturday nights proved a problem: most suitable places had long been booked. We resolved this issue by switching to a luncheon. I found a lovely room for Saturday at the Boca Hotel.

That being settled, my remaining responsibility was momentous. I was ordered to keep the event a secret from Grace. There was no hope of making every aspect a surprise, though. We began with a cover story. Lisa would come down on Tuesday, April 11th with Virginia, who was off from school and had never seen our Dalton Apartment.

Grace saw the dressy outfits that Lisa and Virginia had brought with them. They explained that they wanted to take her to a nice restaurant for a small birthday dinner. This ruse was kept up even after Michael, Elizabeth and Joseph showed up at our door. Lisa and Joseph decamped to a hotel and the McNamara's stayed in our apartment. Joseph Michael squeezed a 36 hour visit between school commitments, arriving Friday night. Lisa and Joseph managed last minute arrangements from out of Grace's hearing.

To maintain the deception, Brigitte called Saturday morning, to wish her Gram Happy Birthday. Our youngest grandchild was uncharacteristically brief, saying she had to play a baseball game that morning in Wyckoff. In reality, Brigitte, Donna and Ray were at a hotel in Boca Raton.

I told Grace there was a new restaurant at the Boca Hotel which we could take the family for lunch. The signs in the hotel lobby, directing guests to the party were hastily removed.

Despite the obstacles, we had pulled it off. Grace's surprise on entering the room was precious. When she saw that the entire family, including the Wyckoff contingent, had made it, she was joyously tearful. Squeezing Brigitte's hand, Grace responded "But you're playing baseball" over and over.

Our friends and family had been summoned to the party by beautiful invitations, created by Joseph and Lisa. Flowers, decorations, music and food were terrific. Part of the entertainment was a slide show chronicling the life of a beautiful princess from Queens as she consorted with a skinny kid from Union City.

The whole day was outstanding. The highlights were captured on video and still pictures by Raymond and Lisa.

CHAPTER TWENTY-SEVEN

Grace's 80th Birthday Plus

As you know from the previous chapter, our family had successfully pulled off Grace's surprise party in Florida on her birthday. Not satisfied with this tribute, our children then decided she should have another party with her New Jersey friends. For this party, I was kept in the dark as well. In the spirit of celebration, they decided to honor my birthday, June 4th and our anniversary July 23rd in the celebration.

The cover story was even more elaborate this time. They sneaked our address book out of the house. For a location, they chose Ridgewood Country Club, although other locations had been discussed. Betty Garino was enlisted to arrange a Sunday afternoon foursome with Grace and me. During that conversation, Betty offered to work her husband Ed's birthday (June 1st) into the ruse.

A round of golf was considered, but the club's maitre d', Louis, pointed out the problems with that plan. If the weather wasn't good, Louis said, I would not agree to play golf. He suggested Sunday brunch instead. When invited, Grace and I thought brunch would be a fine way to celebrate Ed's birthday. It proved fortunate that Betty was the only one who knew the country club didn't have Sunday Brunch.

The pictures that follow will tell you the rest of the story.

CHAPTER TWENTY-EIGHT

Retirement

Whenever the issue of retirement is raised, I insist on defining "retirement". My definition has always been *"retirement is the ability to do what you want to do when you want to do it"*. This assumes good health, of course. Without that, doctors decide what you are going to do. By this definition, I might be retired.

When I was growing up, only government or railroad workers with pensions could retire. Everyone else was expected to work until death or disability. Relatively few people lived past 65 or 70 in the pre-war years.

Social Security came into existence after President Roosevelt's second term began in 1936, but cultural changes were more gradual. Today, the concept of retirement has changed. People can receive full social security benefits at 65, with partial coverage available at 62. A fortunate few can receive pensions as early as age 55. The tax laws were changed to permit IRA and Keogh plans. Medical research has improved so people are living longer and hopefully healthier. These situations require reconciliation of the ability, and in some cases, the necessity to work, with the Social Security programs. Equally important is the preparation for retirement, recognizing the change in income, the needs of food, clothing and shelter, and the time availability.

Food habits will change from the regular business or other luncheon program, the business or political dinners to a more relaxed and less demanding schedule.

Clothing will see the omission of jacket and tie to more casual clothing such as golf or tennis shirts and shorts.

With the family grown and married, the larger multiple bedroom, recreation room, dining and kitchen rooms must be reviewed. As I have said many times we only NEED three rooms: a bedroom, a kitchen (much smaller) a living/recreation room and a bathroom (no long lines for the availability). The large play yard, backyard pools, and lawns and gardens are no longer necessary.

The housing market is now filled by many types of condominium, town houses and, yes, extended living facilities. Country clubs, town and YMCA/YWCA pools provide whatever degree of use you desire. By the time the retirement stage is reached, inevitable signs of wear and tear appear on body and mind. In some cases, people have abused these great gifts of God. Even without such mistreatment, it is (at least) patch and repair time.

All in all, retirement has been very enjoyable. I can wake up whenever I feel like and can decide each day what I want to do. If I want, I can go to the office or stay home, edit video, spend time on the Internet, or play golf with Grace. I can even spin out a tall tale and call it an autobiography. I hope and pray that Grace and I can continue this life between Wyckoff and Florida.

CHAPTER TWENTY-NINE

Creativity

What would an autobiography be without advice? My advice to my grandchildren is that they must give 110% to any task they take on.

In addition, I'd suggest that when they find something they want to do in life, they should seek out others in their chosen fields. People like to share their experience, and anyone who's willing to listen can learn a great deal.

My grandchildren should learn the art of saving part of their income, using whatever plans and schemes ARE available. Grace and I have done well by buying our homes with the aid of mortgages, which provided a form of forced saving. If they begin a family, they should provide for that family's future with term life insurance. If they have children, they should accept that no one can completely plan their children's paths. A good parent can only provide the means to the future, especially education. That education can include college or a trade or business, or all of the above.

In my own life, I can look with pride on my accomplishments. I consider myself a people person, and my choice of law as a career and politics as an avocation provided an enjoyable and fruitful life.

Other than marrying Grace, one of my most important accomplishments was forming the Bergen Bank of Commerce with Frank Rieger and John Gabriel in 1970. Setting up the bank permitted me to use my knowledge of accounting, real estate, taxes and general law, to make decisions as Chairman of the Board of Directors, rather than simply advising others. Even the sale of the bank in 1988 was fortuitous, by providing a substantial retirement fund.

CHAPTER THIRTY

Reflections On The Road Of Life I Traveled

It is 4:00 AM and a little sinus head cold has caused me to come down stairs to have a cup of tea. My mind starts to roll.

In reflecting on this road of life, I realize my first 18 years up through high school might be described as a straight country road (not necessarily paved) with a few bumps. In 1940, the road appears to be a single lane county paved road with extremely different landscaping: the milk business, college, World War II in Europe, and a return home in 1945.

The direction of my trip seems a little better defined after I returned to New York University School of Commerce, the Delta Sigma Fraternity, the Neumann Club and, especially, the intersection with the road of my wife, Grace.

The road from 1945 to1949 is straight and reasonably paved with clear objectives of career and marriage. The marriage introduces a pleasant way with nice scenery: a loving and beautiful wife in our own home with the prospect of my completing law school and Grace continuing to teach.

What might be described as a bump or diversion in the road, God's instructions come forth and Grace becomes pregnant. In June 1950 Virginia was born and we had to take a map out and see where this road was going. With God on your side, the road may require a little slower travel.

I continued to practice accounting, learned the rent control laws in New Jersey, represented small landlords and built my business at a moderate pace. In December 1950, the road signs become a little clearer as I pass the bar and head for a major destination: a husband and father, a provider for my family.

The road from 1950 to probably 1970 may be described as a single lane well paved and well signed road. The development of a law practice, the birth of three girls, the involvement in UNICO and other community organizations, the political parties, etc.

Around 1970, the road became a multiple lane highway, with three daughters embarking on their trips. Up to that point, my story was not too difficult to tell. Now I have to manage my own plus three new trips. I assure you it was an enjoyable time as we looked at the three persons we had given life, take on the challenges facing them.

The first paragraph of this story I referred to my mother. There she was not five feet tall, quietly guiding, directing and supporting this aggressive growing young boy, without the help of a father.

In 1946 another lady entered my life, Grace with the same quite but strong personality; to become my wife and the mother of our children. Throughout the trip she was there, in many times without the materialistic things she deserved, never complaining and always supportive of the road we were traveling.

The three daughters are clearly in my life, "making me believe I was the boss", but affecting all of the turns in the road.

These ladies are all real and in life, but I must never forget the Lady of the Blessed Mother Mary. As my mother and wife in real life were there, I often called upon Her ability to speak to Her Son in my behalf, and am blessed for it.

Born On The Wrong Side Of The Tracks . . .

. . . Realized It Was The Right Side!

Despite the obstacles, we had pulled it off. Grace's surprise on entering the room was precious. When she saw that the entire family, including the Wyckoff contingent, had made it, she was joyously tearful. Squeezing Brigitte's hand, Grace responded "But you're playing baseball" over and over.

Our friends and family had been summoned to the party by beautiful invitations, created by Joseph and Lisa. Flowers, decorations, music and food were terrific. Part of the entertainment was a slide show chronicling the life of a beautiful princess from Queens as she consorted with a skinny kid from Union City.

The whole day was outstanding. The highlights were captured on video and still pictures by Raymond and Lisa.